Boeing-Boeing

A FARCE IN TWO ACTS

by
Marc Camoletti

Adapted by
Beverley Cross

SAMUEL FRENCH

FOUNDED 1830

New York Hollywood London Toronto
SAMUELFRENCH.COM

BOEING-BOEING was first presented February 2, 1965, at the Cort Theatre, N.Y.C., by Martin Lee, by arrangement with Hal Wallis Productions and John Gale Productions Ltd. It was designed by Hutchinson Scott, with supervision and lighting by Lloyd Burlingame. The director was Jack Minster.

CAST
(*In order of appearance*)

JANET	*Diana Millay*
BERNARD	*Gerald Harper*
BERTHA	*Maureen Pryor*
ROBERT	*Ian Carmichael*
JACQUELINE	*Susan Carr*
JUDITH	*Joanna Morris*

The action of the play takes place in Bernard's apartment near Orly Airport in Paris.

ACT ONE

SCENE 1: *Morning*
SCENE 2: *Afternoon*

ACT TWO

Evening

CAST OF CHARACTERS

BERNARD, *a Parisian bachelor*

JANET, *an American air hostess*

BERTHA, *Bernard's housekeeper*

ROBERT, *a friend of Bernard's*

JACQUELINE, *a French air hostess*

JUDITH, *a German air hostess*

The action of the play takes place in Bernard's flat near Orly Airport in Paris.

ACT ONE

ACT TWO

Evening

Boeing-Boeing

ACT ONE

SCENE 1

The living room of BERNARD'S *flat.* BERNARD *and* JANET *are finishing breakfast.*

JANET. (*Sitting* L. *of coffee table.*) Bernard, darling, do you think I've time to eat another pancake?

BERNARD. I should think so—if you hurry. . . . Bertha!

JANET. I adore pancakes for breakfast, don't you?

BERNARD. (*Above table.*) Not especially. I can just about manage a cigarette.

JANET. But back home, all our dieticians agree that a good breakfast prevents day-long neurosis.

BERNARD. If I lived in America I'd probably *have* a day-long neurosis, even with breakfast.

BERTHA. (*Entering.*) Did you call, sir?

BERNARD. Another pancake, Bertha.

BERTHA. (*Crosses to above chair* C. *behind armchair.*) For Miss Janet?

JANET. Please.

BERTHA. And more of that black stuff to pour over it?

JANET. No, thank you. And it's not "black stuff," it's molasses—very good for the complexion.

BERTHA. Well, I don't know what it's for, but I suppose it's alright. I mean, everyone has to get along as best they can. I don't like the look of it myself, but then I'm not here to reform the world.

BERNARD. Well, that's a relief. So just get busy on the pancake.

BERTHA. (*Moves* U.) All right. But don't blame me if it makes her ill.

BERNARD. You're not going to eat it?

BERTHA. No.

BERNARD. So there's no need to argue about it. (BERTHA *crosses to kitchen door.*) Just hurry up—Miss Janet hasn't got much time.

JANET. Please, Bertha. Do hurry. I shall miss my plane.

BERTHA. All right. I'm going. There's no need to shout at me. It's not easy, you know. (*She exits.*)

JANET. That woman's always so bloody-minded.

BERNARD. (*Sits* R. *of table.*) Not really, darling.

JANET. She's becoming a bore.

BERNARD. No. It's just her way. (*Pours out coffee— pot empty.*) Don't worry about it.

JANET. I *do* worry. If it goes on we'll just have to get rid of her, honey.

BERNARD. Whatever for?

JANET. I don't think she likes me.

BERNARD. Now, darling, of course she likes you. It's just that all this food you eat—it seems to upset her. . . . It gives her a sort of indirect indigestion.

JANET. (*Rises—crosses to* BERNARD'S R.) What time is it, darling?

BERNARD. Between a twenty and quarter to ten.

JANET. (*Sighs.*) I don't know . . . when I'm with you time just whistles by.

BERNARD. It's sweet of you to say so.

JANET. It's true. . . . Is it the same for you?

BERNARD. Of course.

(BERTHA *enters to above table.*)

JANET. And does it drag when I'm away?

BERNARD. Terribly. Never ending.

JANET. How marvelous!

BERTHA. Another pancake.

JANET. (*Crosses below to* L. *chair. Sits.*) Thank you, Bertha.

BERTHA. And is that the lot?

BERNARD. No. Some more coffee and another orange juice for Miss Janet.

JANET. No, darling. Truly. I've had enough.

BERTHA. Well, thank the Lord for that! (*She exits with coffeepot.*)

JANET. You see—she doesn't like me.

BERNARD. Darling—

JANET. She doesn't. She's friendly enough when I get home, and when I'm around, she's not too bad. But when it's time to go, she's decidedly hostile—almost anti-American.

BERNARD. Perhaps she's sad because you're going?

JANET. Because I'm your fiancée?

BERNARD. Of course.

JANET. And if I was here all the time, she'd be all right?

BERNARD. Ah! Then we'd all be happy. (*They embrace.*)

JANET. (*Rises.*) I'd better get dressed quickly, or I'll miss the plane.

BERNARD. (*Crosses to desk.*) And that would never do.

JANET. No. It would be terrible.

BERNARD. Terrible. . . . Tell me, darling: When do you get back?

JANET. (*Sits* L. *arm of armchair, still eating pancake.*) Well . . . it's Saturday today . . . we arrive New York at 17.06, then San Francisco—but straight there and back.

BERNARD. And when will you be back in Paris?

JANET. We arrive back in Paris Monday evening. And off again on Wednesday.

BERNARD. (*Checking his timetable.*) Monday . . . what time in the evening, darling?

JANET. 18.30, local time.

BERNARD. Excellent. So whatever happens in San Francisco, you'll be back on Monday?

JANET. That's right.

BERNARD. Good. (*Puts timetable away.*)

JANET. But why do you have to check it in the time-table?

BERNARD. To avoid confusion.

JANET. What confusion?

BERNARD. Darling, I'm a busy man. I've got work to do. I want to make sure that it's all done by the time you get back here so I can spend from Monday to Wednesday with you.

JANET. You're a genius.

BERNARD. I know—it's lovely, isn't it?

JANET. (*Rises to BERNARD D. R.*) I always dreamed of marrying a millionaire, but you're so sweet and considerate that I think you'll do till one turns up.

BERNARD. (*Hands JANET across to bedroom D. R.*) Thank you! And it's a comfort to know that millionaires are in short supply. Now, hadn't you better hurry?

JANET. You want to get rid of me?

(*Enter BERTHA.*)

BERNARD. What do you think? Of course I hate to see you go. But I've got work to do and you've got work to do.

BERTHA. (*Crosses to table from kitchen.*) Here's your coffee.

BERNARD. Thank you.

JANET. Bertie, dear? Will you do me a favor?

BERTHA. Depends. (*Puts cups on tray—folds napkins.*)

JANET. It's Mr. Bernard. Will you take good care of him till I get back on Monday?

BERTHA. I'll do my best. But he's a big boy now, you know.

JANET. But they're all kids at heart.

BERTHA. Kids! Well, thank the Lord there aren't too many like him.

BERNARD. That'll do, Bertha.

BERTHA. She asked me! I'm only expressing an opinion. She asked me my opinion, so I expressed it.

BERNARD. And we're all very grateful. Now get on with it.

(BERTHA *pushes armchair to* R. C. *and thumps cushions.*)

JANET. I'll go and get dressed, uh? (*She exits* D. R. *bedroom.*)

BERNARD. Bertha! Bertha! When I engaged you, you promised never to plump the cushions. It's not that sort of a flat. (*Crosses* R. C.) What's for lunch today?

BERTHA. (*Crosses to* R. *of armchair.*) The American's flying out?

BERNARD. Yes. Well?

BERTHA. You look after the timetables. And the menus change with the timetables. Change all the time! They change.

BERNARD. (*Crosses below to* L. *of table, drinks coffee.*) Now, Miss Jacqueline will be here for lunch.

BERTHA. Miss Jacqueline?

BERNARD. Yes.

BERTHA. Ah! Well, that's all right then. I think I can cope with that one. But it isn't simple, you know. I find it very difficult to keep track of them all. I don't know how you manage it. It isn't easy.

BERNARD. I know it isn't easy. There's no need to keep reminding me.

BERTHA. Well, as long as you appreciate it. That's all I ask, you know. A little appreciation . . . so what do you want for lunch?

BERNARD. You're the cook. You please yourself.

BERTHA. Miss Jacqueline is it? Now I like her. What about a casserole?

BERNARD. (*Crosses to desk with cup, begins looking at timetables.*) We had a casserole last Saturday.

BERTHA. Of course we did. Miss Jacqueline was here last Saturday. She liked it. She told me so. I remember, she said—Bertha, that was very nice. What did you put in it? Just steak, kidney, tomato and mushroom, I said. . . .

(*During* BERTHA's *ad lib:*)

BERNARD. I just thought . . . It occurred to me . . . I was thinking . . . All right. You win. A casserole.

BERTHA. (*Picks up tray—leaving coffeepot.*) And what about dinner? A nice roast? Veal perhaps?

BERNARD. Roast veal? Yes. Excellent.

BERTHA. (*Begins to exit.*) With onions?

BERNARD. Yes—er—no, no, wait a minute. Can't be done.

BERTHA. No onions?

BERNARD. (*Examines his notebook and timetables.*) No. No roast veal either. Near thing that, Bertha. You see it's Miss Jacqueline for lunch, but it's Miss Judith for dinner. She arrives at 19.06.

BERTHA. I see. No need to say any more. No roast veal. Back to sauerkraut and frankfurters. (*Exits.*)

BERNARD. (*Replaces timetable, crosses to table with cup.*) Sorry about that, Bertha. (BERTHA *muttering.*)

JANET. (*Enters in her TWA uniform. Crossing to armchair.*) Darling, is the clock in our room right?

BERNARD. I don't know, darling—but it is nearly ten o'clock.

JANET. (*Sits armchair.*) Then I've just time to do my nails.

BERNARD. Do your nails—but the plane leaves at eleven, darling.

JANET. I can spare two minutes.

BERNARD. (*Crosses to* R. *of* JANET.) Don't blame me then if the traffic's thick, and the lift gets stuck. . . . I really think you ought to get going.

JANET. (*Takes out some nail polish from her shoulder-sack.*) Oh, stop fussing. . . . You know, sweetie, I'm really very happy.

BERNARD. Because you're going?

JANET. Don't be mean. No, I'm happy because I think they're going to transfer me to a new machine.

BERNARD. Really.

JANET. Brand-new. The Super-Boeing. It's just fantastic. Delta wings and four Rolls-Royce turbo-jets. And do you know, darling, each jet has a thrust of nineteen thousand pounds.

BERNARD. Oh, that's interesting.

JANET. You bet it's interesting, and especially for us.

BERNARD. Well, I know you're keen on your job, but I can't see what a thrust of nineteen thousand pounds has to do with me.

JANET. But it'll make the journey so much faster, darling. So I'll be here more often. We can spend more time together.

BERNARD. (*Reflective.*) I see. . . .

JANET. You don't seem very pleased.

BERNARD. Oh! But of course I'm pleased, darling . . . very pleased. But we can't get too excited. I mean, you're not transferring tomorrow . . . (*Anxious.*) . . . are you?

(*A ring at the front door.*)

JANET. Not tomorrow. But soon, very soon.

(BERTHA *enters from kitchen.*)

BERNARD. (*Crosses* L. *to above table.*) Good. Excellent, and if I wanted to be sure of that transfer, I'd make certain of catching this plane. And if you want to get to Orly by eleven, you'll have to go now.

BERTHA. He's right, you know. Better safe than sorry, eh, Mister Bernard? (*Exits main door.*)

BERNARD. You mind your own business and open the door.

JANET. (*Crosses to desk, looking in mirror.*) You're very sweet, and I love you both.

BERNARD. Thank you.

JANET. I'm off across the world. Leaving my little French home behind me. All ready to welcome me when I come back.

BERNARD. You'll find nothing changed.

JANET. I hope not.

BERTHA. (*Enters.*) There's a Mr. Castin to see you . . . a Mr. Robert Castin.

BERNARD. Castin? Castin? I don't know anyone called Castin. Oh! But of course! Show him in. (BERTHA *exits leaving door open.*) We were at school together. Dear old Robert. Haven't seen him for ages.

(BERTHA *enters with* ROBERT.)

ROBERT. (R. *of* BERNARD *below rostrum.*) Well, well, well. . . .

BERNARD. Robert, this is a surprise! You! Here in Paris. I can hardly believe it. How *are* you?

ROBERT. (*Delighted.*) I'm fine, and how are you?

BERNARD. I'm fine and you?

ROBERT. I'm fine.

BERNARD. Dear old Robert!

ROBERT. (*Turns as if to hand coat to* BERTHA, *discovers* JANET *on his right.*) Dear old Bernard! . . . I say, I'm not interrupting anything, am I?

BERNARD. Of course not. An old friend like you. And it must be five years or more since we met.

ROBERT. Four.

BERNARD. Whatever it was, it was much too long. It's good to see you.

ROBERT. Me too. Much too long.

JANET. Bernard!

BERNARD. An old friend of mine. Robert Castin.

JANET. (*Shakes hands.*) How do you do?

ROBERT. Delighted.

BERNARD. Miss Janet Hawkins. American by birth, an air hostess by profession. T.W.A.—as you can see.

ROBERT. My congratulations, Miss Hawkins. And to T.W.A. (*Shakes her hand.*)

JANET. But, Bernard, darling, you've forgotten the important bit.

BERNARD. Yes . . . what bit?

JANET. That we're engaged, honey.

BERNARD. Of course. Robert—this is my fiancée.

ROBERT. (*Turns as if to shake* BERNARD'S *hand, turns back to* JANET *and shakes hands with her.*) Congratulations all round then. Especially you, Bernard. You're a lucky fellow.

BERNARD. Isn't she adorable?

ROBERT. Adorable.

JANET. And your friend Bernard is sweet. So we're all lovely. . . . Are you engaged, Robert?

ROBERT. Alas, no! No, not yet. I'm afraid. I come from Aix, you see; and in the provinces . . . things were much quieter, much quieter.

BERNARD. Quite.

JANET. But there are lots of pretty girls in the South. And you're extremely—

ROBERT. Oh! Extremely. But I've never found one. Still not to worry. Now I'm in Paris, perhaps I'll be luckier. And anyway, you can't be interested in the story of my life. I'm in the way. I'll come back later. . . . (*Moves up to front door.*)

BERNARD. You'll do no such thing.

JANET. (*Crosses up to front door between them.*) Besides, I'm just off.

BERNARD. (*Opens door.*) And about time.

ROBERT. Are you sure? I mean, you're not going just because of me?

JANET. Of course not. I've got to go spread my wings.

ROBERT. Spread your what?

BERNARD. Air hostess.

ROBERT. Oh, wings. Yes, of course.

JANET. (*Crosses* D. *to* ROBERT.) And it's such a pity. You're the first friend of Bernard's I've ever met. He's such a secretive man. I think he hides them all away somewhere.

BERNARD. (*Breaks* D. L.) Not at all. The man lives in Aix. It's not next door, you know.

JANET. Are you going to stay in Paris?

ROBERT. I have to. I'm up on business, you see.

JANET. Wonderful! Then we're bound to meet again.

ROBERT. I shall look forward to that.

JANET. And you can look after Bernard for me till I get back.

ROBERT. If you say so.

BERNARD. Darling, if you don't go soon you won't get back anywhere.

JANET. (*Crosses to* BERNARD.) Don't you rush me. Besides, I've got to give you just one more kiss.

BERNARD. (*To* ROBERT.) All right, old man?

ROBERT. Please. Go ahead. Don't mind me. (*He turns to the mirror and takes off glasses.*)

(JANET *and* BERNARD *embrace.*)

JANET. I adore you.

BERNARD. And I adore you.

JANET. Goodbye, Mr. Castin.

ROBERT. Goodbye. (*Turns, expecting to find* JANET *behind him.*)

JANET. (*To* BERNARD.) You're a darling. An absolute darling.

BERNARD. And you're—you're going to be late. (*Pushing her up to door—opens it.* ROBERT *crosses onto rostrum.*)

JANET. See you Monday.

BERNARD. 18.30—local time. (JANET *blows him a kiss, and exits main door and leaves it open.*)

ROBERT. You rascal! I must say, you've done yourself very well. That's a marvelous girl . . . lovely!

BERNARD. (*Shuts door.*) Yes. She's pretty good.

ROBERT. Much better than that. If I can find myself something half as good, I'll be a happy man.

BERNARD. (*Crosses to desk above.*) Well, let's have a drink on it. . . . What'll it be? Whiskey?

ROBERT. (*Puts coat, hat, umbrella on back of armchair* D. C.) Anything you like. . . . What a lovely girl.

And what a wonderful view from up here. You can see all Paris.

BERNARD. It's all right, isn't it?

ROBERT. (L. *of table*.) Are you still in the architect business?

BERNARD. (*Crossing with drink to above table*.) S⁺ill at it . . . you know. Robert—it's good to see you! It really is.

ROBERT. Well, you always said, "Come and see me when I'm fixed up in Paris" and here you are, all fixed up. And here am I.

BERNARD. (*Back at desk, getting own drink*.) Dear old Robert.

ROBERT. And if you can give me the address of your estate agent, I'm going to fix myself up too—I want a flat just like this. Same layout. Same wonderful view.

BERNARD. (D. R. C.) It's a bit big—for a bachelor—that is.

ROBERT. But I'm going to get married.

BERNARD. You're not!

ROBERT. I am.

BERNARD. But you're not engaged.

ROBERT. Not exactly. (*Crosses to* D. C. *between armchair and table*.) But I do know a girl, well, we're vaguely acquainted, you see. A charming girl really. I haven't actually asked her yet, but I should think it'll be all right. Anyway, I'd like to get married. I can't go on living alone much longer.

BERNARD. You look perfectly all right to me.

ROBERT. Of course I'm all right. So are you for that matter.

BERNARD. You're still a young man.

ROBERT. (*Crosses to* D. L. C.) Well, so are you. You're in good shape, you're young, and you're going to get married.

BERNARD. I most certainly am not.

ROBERT. Not? But I thought . . . well, (*Crosses* U. *between armchair and table to* C.) this delightful American girl, just now . . . she said you were engaged. And you agreed with her. I heard you.

BERNARD. Well, if you want to be technical, I suppose you could say we were engaged. Yes.

ROBERT. Then you're going to get married.

BERNARD. No.

ROBERT. (L. *of* BERNARD.) Look. I may be from the provinces, and I may be a bit slow, but if you're engaged, then you're going to get married. It's not only technical, it's logical! . . . isn't it?

BERNARD. No, it isn't. And besides, why do you want to get married? Do you love this girl?

ROBERT. (*Sits armchair.*) I don't know. I mean, I'm not raving mad about her. I don't write poems or refuse to eat or any of that sort of thing. But it would be nice. I mean, think of the social advantages. They're not to be sneezed at, are they?

BERNARD. I can't think of *one*. Still, if you must get married, get married. But why don't you do it my way?

ROBERT. What way?

BERNARD. (*Bringing desk chair to* R. *of* ROBERT.) The only way. Polygamy.

ROBERT. Polygamy?

BERNARD. It's the ideal life—pleasant, soothing, and it never gets boring. You ought to try it.

ROBERT. Polygamy? You mean lots of wives?

BERNARD. (*Sits.*) Not wives, old man, fiancées. You have all the advantages of married life without any of the inconveniences. Fiancées are much more friendly than wives. And you don't need all that many. I do very well with three.

ROBERT. Three?

BERNARD. It's the ideal number. Less than three would be monotonous. More would be terribly tiring. Three is just perfect.

ROBERT. You're joking.

BERNARD. Not at all.

ROBERT. But it's immoral.

BERNARD. Immoral? But, my dear old Robert, they all think they're the only one. *They* don't think it's immoral, so why should I? All the advantages of a harem right in the middle of Paris, without any of the fuss of becoming a Mohammedan.

ROBERT. But have you considered the hazards? They tell me one wife can drive a man up the wall— What about three!

BERNARD. Not my three.

ROBERT. You may be talented, but you're not invulnerable.

BERNARD. It's just a question of order, old boy. I am organized—beautifully organized. And besides, all my fiancées are working.

ROBERT. I should hope so. If they weren't you'd find it pretty expensive!

BERNARD. I assure you, they cost me no more than one legitimate wife.

ROBERT. (*Sits on* R. *arm of armchair.*) But look here, Bernard . . . isn't it complicated?

BERNARD. Not in the least. All you need is a timetable.

ROBERT. (*Re-sits in armchair.*) I should think you do!

BERNARD. (*Rises to desk, for timetable, back to* C.) You're not quite with me, old man.

ROBERT. No, I'm not.

BERNARD. I mean a special kind of timetable. An airline timetable.

ROBERT. (*Rises to* C. *above armchair.*) To get out in a hurry?

BERNARD. Not at all. Look—here it is. The timetables of all the major airlines—all in one volume. (*Hands timetable to* ROBERT.)

ROBERT. One volume.

BERNARD. You understand?

ROBERT. Yes. . . .

BERNARD. You don't really, do you?

ROBERT. . . . No. . . .

BERNARD. (*Sits* R. *of armchair.*) It's really very simple.

My three fiancées are all recruited from airline personnel. They're all air hostesses.

ROBERT. (*Crosses* D. R. *of armchair.*) Air hostesses?

BERNARD. Yes.

ROBERT. All three?

BERNARD. All three.

ROBERT. Don't be ridiculous. (*Throws timetable at* BERNARD, *then takes it back. He is indignant, then suddenly beams.*) . . . Three air hostesses. What a marvelous idea! (*Sits armchair.*) One up, one down and one pending!

BERNARD. That's all there is to it. And they're all charming.

ROBERT. Well, if your T.W.A. fiancée was anything to go by—charming . . . exquisite!

BERNARD. I promise you—the other two are just as exquisite. I mean, they're already tried and tested. The entrance exams to these companies are really very difficult, you know. Apart from being beautiful, they have to be healthy, good at cooking, good at nursing, witty, wise and friendly. What more could a man want?

ROBERT. I can't think . . .

BERNARD. The only snag is that I have to choose them from different airlines and from different routes—so they don't meet, you see. But that's the only inconvenience.

ROBERT. (*Rises to below table.*) Well, I do take my hat off to you, old chap. The theory's very attractive and I'd be fascinated to see how it works out in practice.

BERNARD. (*Rises to him, collects timetable and crosses to desk.*) And so you shall. You stay here for a week, and you'll see the maestro at work. Now you've already met Janet. That's my American. (*He looks down at his watch.*) Well, Flight X37 touched down ten minutes ago, so in a quarter of an hour you'll meet Jacqueline.

ROBERT. Jacqueline?

BERNARD. Air-France. A little kitten . . .

ROBERT. No!

BERNARD. A real darling. You wait and see. She'll be here for lunch.

ROBERT. Lunch? (*Crosses to* BERNARD D. R.) But that's running it close, isn't it? I mean the other one was here for breakfast. Rather touch and go, isn't it?

BERNARD. Yes, it is touch and go today. It's Saturday, you see, and she was coming from Gander. Generally it works out fairly straightforwardly. Two days Janet, two days Jacqueline, and two days Judith—that's my Lufthansa one.

ROBERT. Ah! It's an international harem?

BERNARD. I was all for the Common Market. (*He brings globe in slightly. Pushes globe to below desk chair.*) Here, I'll show you how it works. Now then, Judith gets in from Stockholm this evening; at the same time, Jacqueline, who has to fly out this afternoon, gets to Cairo, and Janet will be midway between New York and San Francisco . . . you see the work I have to do.

ROBERT. (*Sits desk chair.*) Perpetual motion.

BERNARD. Pure mathematics. Everything organized, regulated and working to the precise second. The earth turns on its axis and my three fiancées wheel above the earth. One this way. One that. One towards the sun. One towards the moon. And eventually they all, in turn, come home to me. No alarms, no surprises. It's geometrical, my dear Robert. So exact as to be almost poetic. And here I sit in the middle—the typical example of polygamous despotism. Perfectly satisfied and healthy—you see. I don't just change my fiancées, I also change my diet. It's like living in a restaurant. So there's no chance of ever getting bored. Neither at table, nor in bed. It's ideal.

ROBERT. Remarkable! (*Rises—to above armchair.*) Qui'e remarkable.

BERNARD. (*Crosses to table below L.*) I must say I do find Janet a bit tricky. These Americans. I don't understand them. All that food they eat and tomato sauce with everything.

ROBERT. She's very pretty.

BERNARD. (*Round above table.*) I find her delightful, but I doubt if I could manage more than two days in the week. Terribly exhausting. But for two days—I've created a dream, old boy, a dream . . .

ROBERT. (*To him.*) But, Bernard . . . where do you find them?

BERNARD. (*Crosses to above desk chair.*) I've a friend who works in the travel agency at Orly Airport and he knows all the air hostesses. He runs little errands for them. They tell him their secrets . . . and if he thinks they're lonely, well, he introduces them to me. (*Takes desk chair back to desk.*)

ROBERT. Does he really?

BERNARD. He might help you. After all he's a friend of mine, I'm a friend of yours . . . I'll give him a ring. (*Lifts telephone.*)

ROBERT. (*Crosses to him.*) Oh, no! No, thank you. This sort of thing's not for me. No. I'm not the type. It's all right for you. You've got the talent, the flair.

BERNARD. That's got nothing to do with it. A time-table's a timetable.

ROBERT. (*Crosses L.*) No! No! Not yet. . . . I'll have to think about it for a couple of years . . . but what happens if they get changed to a different route?

BERNARD. (*To him.*) It's all worked out. It's all on a schedule. Mathematical . . . marvelous!

BERTHA. (*Enters to R. of them.*) Will your friend be here for lunch?

ROBERT. No. No, thank you. I don't want to upset your arrangements.

BERNARD. (*Takes coat to chair by main door.*) Nonsense . . . you're going to stay to lunch, and live with us—till you've found yourself a flat in Paris.

ROBERT. (*Follows* BERNARD *on to rostrum.*) Really, I couldn't. . . .

BERTHA. (*Follows him* U.) He's going to stay?

BERNARD. He is.

BERTHA. And where?

BERNARD. Where do you think? Here, of course.

BERTHA. Which room?

BERNARD. Whichever he likes . . . and fetch my jacket, will you please.

BERTHA. (*To* D. R. *room*.) For goodness sakes, if it isn't one thing it's another. (*She exits to bedroom* D. R. *Both move to above armchair*.)

BERNARD. Where's your luggage?

ROBERT. I left it at the station.

BERNARD. Well, you can pop along later and get it.

BERTHA. (*Returns with* BERNARD'S *jacket. She helps him into it* C. *To* BERNARD.) What time do you want to eat?

BERNARD. As soon as Miss Jacqueline gets here.

BERTHA. That's a lot of help! How long do you think it takes to make a casserole? You don't just rub two sticks together, you know.

BERNARD. It often tastes like it. I'll let you know.

BERTHA. (*To kitchen*.) Mind you do. We can't all make it up as we go along.

BERNARD. All right. I'm sorry. I'll let you know.

BERTHA. (*Turns at door*.) Yes. And there's a letter for the American. From America. It's addressed to a Miss Janet Hawkins.

BERNARD. I'll take it.

(ROBERT U. L. *She gives* BERNARD *the letter*.)

BERTHA. She won't be able to read it till she gets back.

BERNARD. Obviously.

BERTHA. Perhaps someone's died. You wouldn't get *me* to live in America. Not with all those Indians. And don't forget to tell me when Miss Jacqueline gets here. . . . Because of the meat.

BERNARD. I'll send you a smoke signal.

BERTHA. I'm counting on it. You must admit it's a funny sort of life here for a maid.

BERNARD. Don't worry about it, Bertha. And don't

worry about Miss Jacqueline either. She'll be here in good time, especially if she's had the wind behind her.

BERTHA. Right, let's hope Miss Jacqueline has had the wind behind her—'cos the meat's in the oven. (*She exits to kitchen.*)

BERNARD. That woman! (*Replaces globe* D. R.) It's this coming and going, you see. She has to keep changing her style of cooking, and it upsets her a bit.

ROBERT. (*Crosses* L. *of table to* D. C.) Yes, I can understand that. It would rattle anybody. All this traffic . . . and tell me, isn't it at all possible for two of your fiancées to be in Paris at the same time? Just for one night, say?

BERNARD. (*Crosses to* ROBERT, C.) No, impossible—because of the timetables. And even if it did happen, then I'd take the first one out to Saint Germain en Laye or somewhere like that.

ROBERT. First one. Then what happens to number two?

BERNARD. She comes back here.

ROBERT. She comes back here.

BERNARD. Yes, even if Bertha is out, she'd have her own key.

ROBERT. She has her own key?

BERNARD. Yes. They all have their own keys.

ROBERT. They all have their own keys.

BERNARD. And Bertha tells her I've had to go out of town on business. (*Crosses to desk—props letter on ornament.*) Next morning I take number one to the airport, see her aboard a plane, wave my handkerchief, and come back here into the arms of number two. No panic. No problem.

ROBERT. No problem. (*Crosses between table and chair* L. *to above table.*) But the whole thing's rather—well. Don't you love them?

BERNARD. (*To him* C.) But I adore them. I can't do without any of them! I love them so much that if one asks me for something—a tiny present, say—well, I go out and buy three presents! I can't bear to spoil one without spoiling the other two!

ROBERT. That's rather nice. But it still doesn't convince me. I'll settle for a quiet little marriage. Everything ordinary but everything calm.

BERNARD. You're wrong, you know. . . .

ROBERT. (*Sits armchair.*) Maybe. I'm very grateful for your invitation. I accept. First, because I've nowhere else to go, and second, because I'm fascinated to see how you operate.

BERNARD. (*Crosses below and sits L. of table.*) You'll be converted in no time. It's the perfect life, old man. Oh! Just one small point—my three fiancées have the same initial for their Christian names. "J" for Jacqueline, Judith, Janet. It's not essential, but it does help. Slips of the tongue, initials on handkerchiefs—all that sort of thing. (BERTHA *enters from kitchen to* D. R. *door.*) What do you want?

BERTHA. (*Breaks to* R. C.) I don't want anything. I'm just doing my job, that's all. But now the American's gone, I've got to change the room round for Air-France.

BERNARD. Ah yes, of course.

ROBERT. You think of everything?

BERTHA. That's why I'm here, sir. That's my function, you see.

ROBERT. That's your function.

BERTHA. If it wasn't, I don't know what would happen to Mr. Bernard—with all his complications . . . (*She crosses to the bedroom.*) As Miss Jacqueline is only passing through, sir . . . I mean, she's only here for a couple of hours?

BERNARD. (*Rises, crosses above armchair to* BERTHA.) Yes?

BERTHA. Would it be alright if I don't clear up too thoroughly?

BERNARD. No. Just tidy up and change the photographs.

BERTHA. And I'll make up the back room after she's gone, before Lufthansa gets here.

BERNARD. Fine, Bertha. Perfect.

BERTHA. Perfect! Well, I don't know about that. But it cuts down *some* of the work, I suppose. (*She goes out into bedroom* D. R.)

ROBERT. Change the photographs. She must be invaluable.

BERNARD. Yes. She's always muttering, but she does know the routine. It's essential to have someone in the know. Someone to give you a hand in case something goes wrong. Not that it ever does.

BERTHA. (*Enters.*) There you are then.

BERNARD. (*Crosses to her.*) And you haven't forgotten anything?

BERTHA. I don't think so. (*Crossing between them* U. *on rostrum.*)

BERNARD. She'll be here in five minutes.

ROBERT. Such precision!

BERNARD. Precision means efficiency.

BERTHA. I don't know about that. All I know is that when one or other of three young ladies is in transit, then everything gets faster. It's all going to blow up one day, you mark my words. (*Moving to kitchen door.*)

JACQUELINE. (*Enters. She wears the Air-France uniform.*) Darling! (ROBERT *rises to* U. R.)

BERNARD. Darling!

BERTHA. (*Exits. Mutters to* ROBERT.) See what I mean?

BERNARD. Darling, I'd like you to meet my old friend, Robert Castin.

ROBERT. From Aix.

BERNARD. (*Shutting door.*) We were at school together

JACQUELINE. How do you do, Robert?

BERNARD. He's just got in.

ROBERT. How do you do? I just dropped in to see Bernard. We're old friends and we haven't seen each other for ages. He told me you were coming, that he was expecting you. . . . You're sure I'm not in the way?

JACQUELINE. Of course not. I'm delighted—really I am.

You're the first friend of Bernard's I've ever met. He never introduces me to anybody. He's such an old hermit.

ROBERT. Yes. I suppose he is.

JACQUELINE. (*Down to above armchair, puts zip bag on armchair.*) Bernard, darling, fix me a drink, will you? (BERNARD *crosses above her to desk.*) I'm quite worn out. (ROBERT *crosses above her to* L., *looking at her.*) You've no idea how good it is to see the sun—it was ghastly over there. You know we were held up in Gander?

BERNARD. Really?

JACQUELINE. The Met. people forecast a storm, but it was more like a hurricane! Miserable visibility, wind all over the place, and the cloud ceiling was right down to 400 feet. Imagine it!

ROBERT. Delicious.

JACQUELINE. And fog, and so cold! It only cleared over the Channel—but anyway— (*Crosses to* BERNARD—*puts arms round his neck.*) I'm back and that's the main thing . . . have you behaved yourself, darling?

BERNARD. Now what do you think?

JACQUELINE. There's a good boy. (*She turns to* ROBERT.) Has he told you that we're going to get married? (BERNARD *bangs bottle down on desk as warning to* ROBERT.)

ROBERT. He did say he was engaged.

BERNARD. And I also told him you were beautiful. Isn't that what I told you, Robert, old man?

ROBERT. You did. You certainly did.

JACQUELINE. And are you disappointed? (*Breaks in.*)

ROBERT. (*Gallant.*) On the contrary. He wasn't anywhere near the truth.

JACQUELINE. I like your friend, Bernard, darling. He must stay to lunch.

BERNARD. I've already invited him.

JACQUELINE. Wonderful.

ROBERT. I'm afraid I wouldn't like to intrude.

JACQUELINE. Now, not a word. You must do as you're told.

ROBERT. I'd like to do that.

BERNARD. And I've asked him to stay here till he finds himself a flat in Paris.

JACQUELINE. Well done. You'll be company for him.

ROBERT. While you're away?

JACQUELINE. (*Puts glass on* D. *end of desk.*) He's always telling me he's so lonely and complaining that I leave him alone so much . . .

BERNARD. You're so right. When you're not here, I'm absolutely lost!

ROBERT. You poor old chap!

BERNARD. That's what love does for you.

JACQUELINE. Poor darling . . . is lunch ready?

BERNARD. It always is.

JACQUELINE. Well, you may be lonely but you're a born organizer. I adore you.

BERNARD. I just like everything to be shipshape.

JACQUELINE. (*Moves to rostrum, stops.*) You're marvelous. I'll just clean up and then we'll eat. (BERNARD *crosses* C.) I've just three hours before we take off for Cairo! (*Returns to armchair for handbag, crosses up to* C. *of rostrum.*) And that reminds me. You know what? They're putting the Super-Caravel on our route. She's terribly fast, so I'll be able to see you more often.

BERNARD. That's very interesting. You must remember to let me have the new timetables.

JACQUELINE. Of course, darling. I won't be a minute. (*She exits into the bathroom.*)

ROBERT. (*To him.*) If the planes get any faster, your geometry's going to get a bit bent.

BERNARD. Oh! These things take time. It won't all happen at once.

ROBERT. Well, anyway—my congratulations. I was trying to work out which one is the prettier; but it's quite impossible.

BERNARD. Not your problem, old man. They're both engaged. ·

ROBERT. They're both engaged!

(*The TELEPHONE RINGS.* BERNARD *picks it up.*)

BERNARD. (*Crosses to desk.*) . . . Hello. . . . Yes.
. . . What? Oh yes— (ROBERT *sits armchair.*) Where?
Stockholm? Hello, darling! (*He whispers to* ROBERT.)
It's Judith—Lufthansa. (ROBERT *rises, crosses to* BER-
NARD—*hovers anxiously on rostrum to* L. *and* R.) Yes,
darling.

ROBERT. But you've got one in there.

BERNARD. You are going to be back at . . . 23.00 in-
stead of 19.00. What a shame. Yes, I've got that. . . .
What was that? . . . Oh . . . you'll eat on the plane.
Right. . . . Of course, darling . . . and I adore you.

(ROBERT *now at dining-room door.* BERTHA *enters from
kitchen.* ROBERT *jumps.*)

BERTHA. (*To him.*) Mr. Bernard. (*Sees* BERNARD *on
phone, turns to exit to kitchen.*)

BERNARD. (*On telephone.*) Alright, 23.00 hours local
time. . . . Goodbye, darling . . . (*He replaces the telephone.*) Ah! Bertha. Just in time. Cancel the frankfurters.

BERTHA. Lufthansa's delayed?

BERNARD. Stuck in Stockholm.

BERTHA. What a pity. I've bought the sauerkraut, you
see.

BERNARD. Never mind. It'll keep.

BERTHA. Well, if you want to throw your money about.
And another thing . . .

BERNARD. Well?

BERTHA. I've been meaning to speak up for some time.

BERNARD. Out with it then.

BERTHA. I've forgotten what it is now. It's all this coming and going. (*Exits to kitchen.*)

JACQUELINE. (*Enters from the bathroom. To* C.) Was
that the telephone?

BERNARD. Yes.

JACQUELINE. It wasn't for me?

BERNARD. (*Crosses to her with drink.*) No . . . why? Were you expecting someone?

JACQUELINE. (*Sits armchair.*) They may make a change in the flights—because of the weather. They've already canceled the Viscount to Beirut.

ROBERT. (*To R. of her.*) It must be interesting to be in on all that.

BERNARD. (*Sits coffee table.*) They won't alter your flight, will they, darling?

JACQUELINE. No. Instead of leaving at 15.00, we'll take off at 16.00.

BERNARD. (*Pauses—thinking of flight schedules.*) Good.

JACQUELINE. Why do you say "good"?

BERNARD. Did I say good?

ROBERT. Yes, you did say good.

BERNARD. Well, I said "good" because . . . because I instantly realized it would mean an extra hour with you.

JACQUELINE. Oh! You're so sweet . . . so who was it then?

BERNARD. Who was who?

JACQUELINE. On the telephone. . . . It wasn't another woman?

BERNARD. (*Takes her hand.*) Darling, how on earth could it be another woman! I adore you. Don't I, Robert?

ROBERT. Of course you do.

JACQUELINE. Cross your heart?

BERNARD. But, Jacqueline darling, don't be silly about this! It upsets me.

ROBERT. You've gone quite pale, old chap.

BERNARD. (*Rises to U. C.*) You see! I'm pale!

JACQUELINE. (*Rises to desk, glass down on desk, looks in mirror.*) All right . . . so you can tell me.

BERNARD. Tell you what?

JACQUELINE. Who was it on the telephone?

BERNARD. Who was what, darling?

JACQUELINE. On the telephone.

BERNARD. It was . . . it was the wrong number.

ROBERT. Yes, that's it. A wrong number. Some old lunatic. They drive you mad. . . .

JACQUELINE. (*Sees the letter. Picking up letter.*) And what's this?

BERNARD. What's what?

JACQUELINE. This letter . . . it's addressed to Miss Janet Hawkins?

(ROBERT *crosses* L. *with embarrassment.*)

BERNARD. (*Crosses to* JACQUELINE.) Letter? I haven't had a letter.

JACQUELINE. It's here. On your desk.

BERNARD. Nothing to do wi.h me, darling. I've been talking to Robert.

ROBERT. I've only just got here—only just arrived.

BERNARD. All the time.

JACQUELINE. And it just appeared from nowhere?

BERTHA. (*Enters from kitchen. To* R. *of* BERNARD.) I've just remembered what it was.

BERNARD. Good.

BERTHA. Ah! Good morning, Miss Jacqueline.

JACQUELINE. Morning, Bertha.

BERNARD. (*To* BERTHA.) What is it you've just remembered, Bertha?

BERTHA. Lunch is ready.

JACQUELINE. Thank you— Oh, Bertha, what's this?

(BERNARD *and* BERTHA *cross slowly* D., *in step together.*)

BERTHA. A letter.

JACQUELINE. I can see that. But it's addressed to a Miss Janet Hawkins. Do you know her?

BERTHA. (*Crosses* BERNARD, *takes letter, sniffs at it.*) Never heard of her.

JACQUELINE. Well, what's it doing here? (BERTH *turns to* BERNARD *who mimes instructions.*)

BERNARD. Well, Bertha?

BERTHA. Ah! Yes! . . . I've just remembered. The old fool downstairs—the concierge—he muttered something this morning. Said I'd taken a letter belonging to someone else in the block. By mistake, you see.

BERNARD. There.

ROBERT. (*To them.*) Wrong number . . . I mean, wrong address.

BERNARD. Quite . . . simple, really. Everything worked out. . . .

ROBERT. (*Breaks* L.) Everything explained . . . rather neatly, I thought.

BERTHA. My mistake all along. I'm sorry, sir. Sorry, Miss Jacqueline.

BERNARD. We all make mistakes, Bertha.

BERTHA. We're only human after all. Well, some of us are, I suppose. . . . You give it to me, miss, I'll slip it downstairs after lunch. Well, it's all ready when you want it. Lunch, that is. (*Crosses up to kitchen door.*)

JACQUELINE. Thank you, Bertha. You're a marvel. You run the flat as if it were your own.

BERTHA. I do my best, miss. I do try. But—well, you wouldn't understand—but it isn't easy. (*Exits to kitchen.*)

BERNARD. (*To* JACQUELINE.) It isn't easy, but we do try, my darling. You arrive, you wash your hands, have a drink, and—hey, presto!—lunch is ready. All you have to do is to sit down and enjoy it.

ROBERT. (*Crosses* C.) What a life!

JACQUELINE. (*Crosses to between them.*) You're right, Robert dear. You ought to try it. Copy Bernard. Find yourself a fiancée.

ROBERT. Yes, as a matter of fact—I've been thinking about it—quite seriously.

JACQUELINE. (*Looks at her watch.*) Goodness, it's already twenty-five to. We must hurry. Let's have lunch. (*Exits into the dining room.* BERNARD *follows her on to rostrum* R. *then crosses to* C.)

BERNARD. (*Crossing to* ROBERT.) Well, old man. You see how it's done?

ROBERT. I'm lost in wonder.

BERNARD. You just follow me. You can't go wrong. Come and have lunch—French cooking today.

ROBERT. That Air-France uniform. You know, it's beautifully cut. It's really very handsome.

BERNARD. Well, that's the trouble. I never could resist a uniform!

ROBERT. That's the difference between us. You always did move with the times. Cigarettes in bed at school and now air hostesses. And I never got beyond train spotting.

BERNARD. You'll soon get the hang of it, old boy. It's just a question of timetables.

JACQUELINE. Bernard!

BERNARD. Coming, darling. Prepare for take-off.

ROBERT. Bernard—chocks away! (*They exit laughing.*)

CURTAIN

ACT ONE

SCENE 2

The TELEPHONE RINGS. BERTHA *enters and lifts the receiver.*

BERTHA. (*To phone.*) Hello. . . . Yes, that's right. . . . No, Mr. Bernard has gone out. I'm Bertha. . . . Oh! It's you, Miss Judith! You're in Paris? Already. . . . Yes, you are early. Yes, I'm sure he'll be delighted. A little surprise for him? I should think it will be. . . . Well then, see you later. (*Rings off, shakes her head and goes to exit* U. *when the DOORBELL suddenly RINGS. She crosses to door,* U. C.) Who on earth can that be? It's no life for a maid . . . no life for anyone. (*Exits to front door.*)

ROBERT. (*Off.*) It's only me.

BERTHA. (*Off.*) Oh. It's you, Mr. Robert.

ROBERT. (*To* L. *of door with three suitcases and rug bundle.*) There was a queue a mile long at the station. I've never seen so many people—I don't know where they all come from—it's much more peaceful back home.

BERTHA. (R. *of him.*) If all you people stayed at home there wouldn't be such a queue at the station.

ROBERT. No, I suppose not.

BERTHA. And what do you want with all these bags? (*Closes door.*) I thought you were only up here on business.

ROBERT. (*Puts luggage down, retains rug bundle.*) I always believe in being prepared.

BERTHA. I bet you weren't prepared for this place.

ROBERT. No. I wasn't.

BERTHA. And I hope you're not going to stay here too long.

ROBERT. Well, really . . .

BERTHA. (*Wanders* R.) I'm only telling you for your own good. Just you wait and see, people coming and going all the time. You'd have been better off at the station and there'd have been more room for your bags!

ROBERT. (*Crosses down above table.* BERTHA *follows him.*) Well, look. I have been invited and by your . . .

BERTHA. It's not a hotel, you know.

ROBERT. Everything seems to be beautifully organized.

BERTHA. That's just it. It's too well organized. Shall I tell you what I think?

ROBERT. (*In slightly.*) Well . . .

BERTHA. It's not human! That's what I think. (*Crosses* R., *sits desk chair.*) It's all very well for Mr. Bernard giving out invitations left, right and center, but I have to do all the work; what with you and your luggage and now the Lufthansa.

ROBERT. What about the Lufthansa?

BERTHA. She's just rung up to say she's on her way.

ROBERT. Well, that's all right, isn't it? Air-France has just taken off.

BERTHA. I know, but the Lufthansa wants to stay three days.

ROBERT. Oh.

BERTHA. Well, it's nothing to do with me, of course. But Miss Janet—that's the T.W.A. one . . .

ROBERT. Yes, I know, I've met that one.

BERTHA. Well, she's coming back on Monday.

ROBERT. (*Crosses to luggage.*) Not to worry. It's only Saturday. Mr. Bernard will have plenty of time to work something out. . . . Now where would you like me to put these?

BERTHA. (*Rises to above armchair.*) You put them where you like. No, wait a minute, you'd better have that one—that's Mr. Bernard's room. It's quieter back there. You just make yourself at home.

ROBERT. Thank you. That's very kind of you. (*Crosses to U. L. room and exits with rug.*)

BERTHA. Don't thank me. I've got enough to do, thank you very much, without being kind to everybody. I tell you this place is a madhouse.

ROBERT. (*At door.*) If you don't like it why don't you change your job?

BERTHA. What good would that do? You change your boss, and you find that the next one's as bad as the first.

ROBERT. (*To luggage.*) You really are an optimist.

BERTHA. I'm glad you've noticed. It's true . . . (*Sits armchair.*) I'm a cheerful soul at heart. I like a bit of fun, but this place goes too far. But what can you expect in domestic service? I mean there's no dignity in being a maid.

ROBERT. I wouldn't say that . . . well . . . if you'll excuse me I'll get settled in. (*Exits to U. L. bedroom with two suitcases.*)

BERTHA. Yes—you stick them in there. I'd help you with them myself, but when I was a little girl the doctor told my mother . . . (ROBERT *re-enters, picks up suitcase.*) "She's a great tryer, your daugh'er, but not strong, she must be very careful not to lift anything."

ROBERT. Not to lift anything. (*Exits with suitcase—heavy.*)

BERTHA. So I try to be careful. And when you think about it, the body's not much of a thing, is it? Very feeble. It gets tired. It wears out.

ROBERT. (*Re-enters, sits chair L., gets newspaper out of pocket.*) Quite. It does indeed. It does indeed.

BERTHA. So, I let other people wear themselves out.

ROBERT. (*Sits L. chair.*) I see what you mean. . . . I expect I shall be seeing you later.

BERTHA. Oh, I'm boring you.

ROBERT. No, of course not.

BERTHA. Oh yes, I'm boring you. When people say, see you later, it always means they've had enough.

ROBERT. No, I assure you.

BERTHA. I'm getting on your nerves.

ROBERT. Nonsense.

BERTHA. Yes. I'm getting on your nerves.

ROBERT. (*Crosses to desk, pours out drink.*) You are not getting on my nerves.

BERTHA. You don't have to apologize. Mr. Bernard's exactly the same. And there isn't any ice.

ROBERT. What?

BERTHA. I'm defrosting the fridge.

ROBERT. My heartiest congratulations.

BERTHA. Are you in the same business as Mr. Bernard?

ROBERT. No.

BERTHA. Perhaps you're married?

ROBERT. No. I'm not.

BERTHA. You ought to be.

ROBERT. Why?

BERTHA. Well, you're still quite nice.

ROBERT. Thank you.

BERTHA. You take my advice, you get married while you're still worth it.

ROBERT. (*Crosses below table to chair L.*) I intend to, but now I've seen Mr. Bernard I think I'll wait a bit.

BERTHA. (*Measuring him knowingly.*) I don't quite

know what's in your mind, but this sort of life's not for you, you're not the type— To live like him you have to be very dextrous—you have to have your wits about you.

ROBERT. (*Sits chair* L.) And what makes you think . . . ?

BERTHA. I can see it. You see, I can read you with the naked eye, if you'll pardon the expression.

ROBERT. Well, I think I'd better go into the other room. (*Rises with glass to* U. L. *bedroom.*) If you'll excuse me. I'll just take a little rest.

BERTHA. (*Rises to* C. *rostrum.*) You'll get no rest in this place, I can tell you. You take my tip and get married before it's too late. (ROBERT *shuts door.*) I know when I'm not wanted. (*Exits.*)

JUDITH. (*Enters from the hall. She is in the uniform of an air hostess of Lufthansa. Puts hat and bag and gloves on desk.*) Bernard Liebling! . . . Berta!

BERTHA. (*Returns.*) Ah, Miss . . . ? (JUDITH *turns round.*) . . . Judith. (*To* L. *of her.*) You're here already.

JUDITH. I came as fast as I could. If you know how happy I was to be home.

BERTHA. I can see that.

JUDITH. Mr. Bernard isn't in?

BERTHA. No, no. . . . He's gone out . . . on business.

JUDITH. (*Disappointed.*) Oh!

BERTHA. But he'll be back in a minute.

JUDITH. Are you sure?

BERTHA. Certainly. It's nothing very serious. He went out just before you telephoned. . . .

JUDITH. (*In to her.*) And is he happy?

BERTHA. Oh, yes, he's marvelously happy. You know how much he looks forward to seeing you.

JUDITH. Do you think he loves me as much as I love him?

BERTHA. Well, now, that I don't know. I mean, how could I know a thing like that?

JUDITH. (*Crosses to* U. *of armchair.*) Doesn't he talk about me when I'm not here?

BERTHA. Oh, yes, yes, he never stops talking about you, but I can't tell you if he loves you as much as you love him, if I don't know how much you love him. . . .

JUDITH. But, Bertha, darling. You know I adore him.

BERTHA. Then that's all right. He adores you.

JUDITH. And I've got three whole days this time. Isn't that wonderful?

BERTHA. (*Doubtfully.*) Wonderful. . . .

JUDITH. Mr. Bernard will be pleased.

BERTHA. I can't wait to see his face.

JUDITH. (*Wanders to below table, then behind* L. *chair.*) You can't realize how marvelous it is to be back. It seems ages since I've seen him. Though I think of him all the time. In Melbourne. In Ankara, in Colombo, I am always dreaming of our little flat, and my little Bernard sitting all alone thinking of me.

BERTHA. It's beautiful.

JUDITH. (*Above armchair.*) And when we're up about 19 or 20,000 feet, roaring away at 600 miles an hour, and if I've nothing to do, I sometimes wander off into the luggage hold.

BERTHA. (*Thrilled.*) Really.

JUDITH. (*To her.*) I'm all alone there, you see. And I look out of the little porthole at the stars dancing and the moon out there in the sky . . . and I say to myself that my Bernard is looking at them too. (*Taking jacket off.*) And I feel as though we are looking into each other's eyes across the layers of planets and meteorites and the nebulae. . . . I'm madly romantic, you see.

BERTHA. I'm sure you are. Madly.

JUDITH. And does he do that too? (*Jacket down on armchair.*)

BERTHA. What?

JUDITH. S'are at the moon while I'm away.

BERTHA. Oh, I'm sure he does. . . . Mind you, I'm not always there when he's doing it.

JUDITH. I suppose not. Perhaps he prefers to keep it a secret.

BERTHA. And I should hope so. I mean life's complicated enough without dragging in the nebulae.

JUDITH. (*To her, sits on back of armchair.*) But you understand these things, don't you, Berta? I always like talking to you. You know about life. . . . You are a woman.

BERTHA. I'm more than that, miss, I'm a domestic servant. And believe me, Miss Judith, we domestic servants get to know a great deal. . . . And what we know we keep to ourselves—we never say anything . . . mind you, very few people ever ask us.

JUDITH. Oh, but you're something very special, Berta.

BERTHA. You really think so?

JUDITH. (*Crosses below* BERTHA *to* D. R.) I am certain. You are the virgin in the legend of the Grail in the story of the Niebelungen.

BERTHA. Yes. Well, I've been called worse.

JUDITH. You're a guardian. You keep me alive in Bernard's thoughts. You keep the flame of love burning in his heart!

BERTHA. I do?

JUDITH. (*Sits desk chair.*) You're like me—capable of great passion.

BERTHA. It's very nice of you to say so.

JUDITH. I love him so much! Every time I come back, I seem to love him more, and every time I go it just tears me to pieces.

BERTHA. You're very intense, aren't you?

JUDITH. I'm worse than that . . . I'm passion itself. (*Crosses below armchair to* D. L.) But I got carried away, you see. . . . But I just can't keep still. I must do something.

BERTHA. Why don't you have a drink? Something to cool you down. . . . Or a cigarette? To calm you?

JUDITH. A cigarette.

BERTHA. (*Breaks* U. *on entrance.*) I'll get you some.

JUDITH. (*Crosses above to desk, collects bag.*) You're a darling, Berta. I'll get settled in while I'm waiting.

. . . I'm mad with happiness, Berta, just mad with happiness!

BERTHA. And so am I, miss, so am I!

(JUDITH *exits into the* D. R. *bedroom and closes the door as* BERTHA *goes out of hall door. Enter* ROBERT *from the* U. L. *bedroom carrying a copy of* Le Provencal. *He sits down in armchair, opens the newspaper.* JUDITH *comes out of the second bedroom and not recognizing* ROBERT *throws herself at him. Sitting on his lap she kisses him.*)

ROBERT. I say . . .

JUDITH. Oh, I beg your pardon.

ROBERT. My fault entirely.

JUDITH. What are you doing in my flat?

ROBERT. Yours? Don't you mean Bernard's?

JUDITH. If you like. But it's still mine : . . mine or Bernard's, it's the same thing.

ROBERT. I'm an old friend of Bernard's.

JUDITH. (*Rises to* R. *of him. Cold.*) Really?

ROBERT. An old school friend.

JUDITH. How lovely for you.

ROBERT. My name's Robert. Robert . . . I've forgotten my name . . . Robert Castin.

JUDITH. How do you do?

ROBERT. How do you do? (*Rises. They shake hands stiffly.*) And you must be Judith?

JUDITH. (*Warming.*) He's told you about me?

ROBERT. Told me! My dear girl, it's Judith this, Judith that; here, there, everywhere, and all the time. It's Judith . . . Judith . . . all the time.

JUDITH. How divine.

ROBERT. He hardly mentions anything else—well, hardly.

JUDITH. (*Crosses to below table.*) But why are you all on your own?

ROBERT. Well—er—Bernard's just gone out.

JUDITH. (L. *of* L. *chair*.) On business.

ROBERT. (*Moving* U.) That's it! Yes . . . on business. And he told me to wait for him. I just dropped in, you see . . . this morning . . . from the Provinces . . . from Aix.

JUDITH. From Aix.

ROBERT. Yes.

JUDITH. (*Delighted*.) It's not true!

ROBERT. Oh! Yes . . . this morning . . . from Aix.

JUDITH. But that's marvelous!

ROBERT. Is it?

JUDITH. My mother lives in Aix.

ROBERT. She doesn't.

JUDITH. She's lived there for years.

ROBERT. What an extraordinary coincidence.

JUDITH. (*Sits* L. *of table*.) Extraordinary.

ROBERT. Quite extraordinary.

JUDITH. Whereabouts do you live in Aix?

ROBERT. Near the station. Number 27.

JUDITH. It's not true! The Bahnhofstrasse!

ROBERT. The what?

JUDITH. The Bahnhofstrasse.

ROBERT. Oh! The Bahnhof! . . . You mean the station.

JUDITH. You must know my mother's house. It's on the corner of the Friedenstrasse.

ROBERT. The Frieden—what?

JUDITH. Friedenstrasse.

ROBERT. I don't think I know that one.

JUDITH. But you must. It's the next street down from the Bahnhofstrasse.

ROBERT. Is it?

JUDITH. Now don't pretend you don't know it.

ROBERT. (*Sits armchair*.) I can't even pronounce it. I'll get it. It's this Bahnhof that keeps throwing me.

JUDITH. Well, you know the corner? Where Napoleon is?

ROBERT. (*Squats* R. *of table*.) Napoleon the grocer?

JUDITH. You're not trying. No—the chap on a horse. Napoleon. A statue.

ROBERT. A statue? A big statue.

JUDITH. Enormous.

ROBERT. (*Rises to* C.) Well, I'm sorry. But the only statue I've seen is the one of Louis 16th.

JUDITH. Louis 16th.

ROBERT. And he hasn't got a head, let alone a horse.

JUDITH. (*Rises to* L.) Now you're mocking me.

ROBERT. My dear young lady, I assure you . . . Look, I've lived in Aix all my life. We all have. Me, my father, my grandfather, my great-grandfather . . . ask anybody. My grandfather made olive oil, out of olives. My father made it out of almonds. And I make it out of practically anything. It's a sort of progression, you see. We are very respectable and terribly well known. You say you know the place—well, I know everything and everybody in Provence.

JUDITH. Provence?

ROBERT. Yes. Aix is in Provence, isn't it?

JUDITH. But I was talking about Aix-la-Chapelle.

ROBERT. I was talking about Aix en Provence.

JUDITH. Obviously.

ROBERT. So we are both from Aix, but not the same Aix.

JUDITH. I suppose so. I'm really very sorry.

ROBERT. It's too disappointing. . . . You would have made a charming neighbor.

JUDITH. (*Sits* L. *of table.*) You're very kind.

ROBERT. No, truly . . . Miss . . .

JUDITH. You can call me Judith . . . because you're a friend of Bernard's.

ROBERT. And I'm Robert Castin.

JUDITH. I shall call you Robert.

ROBERT. What a good idea. How do you do. (*Shakes hands.*)

JUDITH. How do you do.

ROBERT. Well, then, now we've sorted that out. It's like I was saying— (*Sits armchair.*) Bernard said he could put me up for a few days. I do hope that won't put you out.

JUDITH. But of course not. It's marvelous that Bernard will have someone to talk to. It'll seem less lonely for him.

ROBERT. While you're away.

JUDITH. Yes, that's right. . . . You won't say anything to him about me kissing you, will you?

ROBERT. Oh, but it was all a mistake.

JUDITH. A mistake maybe, but I did kiss you.

ROBERT. Believe me, I won't say a word.

JUDITH. You're very kind.

ROBERT. And anyway, a mistake like that, well . . . it doesn't really count, you know. It was so sudden. I've forgotten about it already.

JUDITH. Didn't it mean anything, then?

ROBERT. You didn't give me much time. And there was no anticipation and I think that's very important. So . . .

JUDITH. (*Cautious.*) So . . .

ROBERT. In order to ensure my complete silence and my absolute discretion, perhaps you'd better give me another one.

JUDITH. (*Rises to* D. L.) A bribe?

ROBERT. No, no, a kiss.

JUDITH. But I'd never forgive myself.

ROBERT. Why ever not? You're Bernard's fiancée. And when you get married you have to kiss all his friends. Especially me—I'm bound to be his best man.

JUDITH. I won't have to kiss you on the lips.

ROBERT. You think not?

JUDITH. (*Crosses to above chair* L.) I'm certain.

ROBERT. Ah! But in America . . .

JUDITH. I'm German.

ROBERT. Yes, yes, of course, that's quite true.

JUDITH. And anyway, when the bride kisses the friends of the groom, it's in front of her husband. He's there watching.

ROBERT. I don't think that's quite fair, do you? There

are particular circumstances. (JUDITH *crosses above* ROB-ERT *to* D. R.) Ours for example.

JUDITH. (*Crosses* D. R.) I don't see that our case is so special. In fact, I think we should both feel very guilty. We are all alone in my fiancé's flat . . .

ROBERT. (*Rises to her.*) Oh, come on. You don't have to make a tragedy out of it. It's not Wagner, you know. It was only a kiss.

JUDITH. So why are you making such a fuss about it yourself?

ROBERT. Well, because . . . because . . . you made rather a happy mistake, you're really very charming, and because we both come from Aix.

JUDITH. But not the same one. Not the same one at all! Aix-la-Chapelle . . .

ROBERT. Aix. All we seem to talk about is Aix. Can't you see this perfectly innocent kiss would be rather unique?

JUDITH. It would be the second.

ROBERT. I don't count the first.

JUDITH. (*Turns her back.*) You really are awful.

ROBERT. Well, you see, Judith, you're the first German girl I've ever met. And I think you're awfully sweet. (*Tries to take her hand which she unconsciously withdraws.*)

JUDITH. Well, maybe . . . (*Turns to him.*) but I am engaged to Bernard, after all.

ROBERT. That makes it worse. I mean you won't get another chance. And nor will I. If we lived in America we could kiss each other without a second's thought, and if it wouldn't be wrong in America, why should it be wrong here? (*Breaks to above armchair.*) After all, America's a great country.

JUDITH. (*To him. Proud.*) So is Germany. (*Kisses him. To* D. R. *room.*) You see? We're a great country too. . . .

ROBERT. You crept up on me again. I wasn't expecting it. You're leaving me all alone?

JUDITH. (*At door.*) And why not? You come in here, insult Germany, tell me all sorts of lies about America—

ROBERT. Not lies . . . not really. Anyway, if you thought they were lies, why did you kiss me again?

JUDITH. Because you are a friend of Bernard's, because I love Bernard, and because your eyes go down at the ends. . . . See you later. (*Exits.*)

ROBERT. (*Crosses to* D. R. *door.*) Judith!

BERTHA. (*Comes in with the cigarettes from the front door.*) Here they are.

ROBERT. Who?

BERTHA. (*To* L. *of him.*) The cigarettes for Miss Judith. By the way, I forgot to tell you—she's arrived, Lufthansa.

ROBERT. I know that. I've seen her.

BERTHA. Good. Is she in her room?

ROBERT. Yes.

BERTHA. Good. (*Step toward him.*)

ROBERT. No, it's all right. I'll give them to her.

BERTHA. (*Sly.*) Ah! Ah!

ROBERT. What do you mean, "Ah, Ah, Ah"? Please be good enough to give me those cigarettes.

BERTHA. You've introduced yourselves then, have you?

ROBERT. Twice.

BERTHA. (*Gives him the cigarettes.*) Then I suppose it's alright if you give her the cigarettes.

ROBERT. Of course it's alright. (*Crosses to door.*) Alright, Bertha, I can manage. I can manage a whole packet all by myself. . . . Haven't you got anything to do?

BERTHA. Well, as a matter of fact, at this particular minute I haven't.

ROBERT. Don't just stand there. You'll get cramp. (*Crosses above* BERTHA *to above table.*)

BERTHA. You'd like me out of the way.

ROBERT. You see . . .

BERTHA. I see very well. I see you want me to go away.

ROBERT. No . . . I don't care what you do. . . . (*Throws cigarettes on table.*) But as there's nothing to do here . . . now . . .

BERTHA. Nor anywhere else.

ROBERT. All right! Go somewhere else and do it there. Go and stand by the fridge with the door open. What are you waiting for?

BERTHA. (*Toward kitchen.*) Nothing . . . it's like I said, there's nothing. Nothing at all . . . nothing . . . nothing. (*Exits through swing door of kitchen. Re-enters on inward swing of door.* ROBERT *has lunged for cigarettes on her exit—falls forward with surprise on her re-entrance.* ROBERT *crosses to* D. R. *door and knocks.*)

JUDITH. (*Off.*) What is it?

ROBERT. I've got something for you.

JUDITH. (*Off.*) No . . . I'm having a little rest . . . please leave me alone.

ROBERT. But I've got your cigarettes.

JUDITH. (*Off.*) Oh! Oh! All right . . . you'd better come in. (*He goes in, leaving the door open.*)

ROBERT. (*Off.*) American cigarettes. (*A pause. Both re-enter.*)

JUDITH. Robert, please! You're not going to start all over again.

ROBERT. But, Judith . . . I've got nothing else to do. (*Both exit.*)

JUDITH. (*Off.*) You seem to have no sense of dignity. (*Pushes him back onstage, slams door, just as* BERNARD *appears with* JACQUELINE.)

(BERNARD *enters—exits to hang up his hat in hall—re-enters.*)

BERNARD. We've come back.

ROBERT. Come back?

JACQUELINE. (*To above table.*) Yes, they suddenly decided to transfer me to the Super-Caravelle, and she's not going into service until tomorrow.

ROBERT. Tomorrow?

JACQUELINE. That's good news, isn't it?

ROBERT. Marvelous news . . . yes.

BERNARD. (U. C.) So we've come back.

ROBERT. Yes.

BERNARD. (*To him.*) So what's the matter?

(JACQUELINE *puts bag on table, takes gloves off, puts in bag.*)

ROBERT. The matter?

BERNARD. Yes, old man, you look worried.

ROBERT. Worried? But I'm not worried. Are you worried?

BERNARD. No.

ROBERT. You will be.

BERNARD. (*Crosses in.*) It's all right, old man. I'll get her out before Judith arrives.

JACQUELINE. (*To* L. *of* BERNARD.) Aren't you pleased to see me?

ROBERT. Of course I am. I am delighted to see you.

JACQUELINE. We can spend the evening together. . . . (*Embraces* BERNARD.) And I'll have the whole night with my darling Bernard.

BERNARD. Well, I don't know about that. . . . I was just thinking it might be fun to go away for the night—to Saint-Germain-on-Laye, perhaps.

ROBERT. An absolutely marvelous idea. Come on, let's go. (*Crosses onto rostrum.*)

JACQUELINE. But why Saint-Germain? (*Crosses back to them* D. R.)

BERNARD. It would make a nice change for you.

JACQUELINE. But I'm perfectly happy here.

ROBERT. Of course you are . . . but the country . . . it's so pretty . . . and the air's so good at Saint-Germain . . . one can really breathe there. (*Demonstrates.*)

JACQUELINE. No! It would be awfully mean to leave you here all alone on your first day in Paris.

ROBERT. (*Taking each of them by the arm he pushes them out of front door and closes it—crosses to* D. R. *door.*) Oh, don't worry about me. You go. I'm just an old hermit. I'm used to it. Just you hurry off and enjoy your-selves.

BERNARD. (*Re-enters, leaving door open, to* R. C. *of rostrum.* JACQUELINE, C.) No hurry, we'll go after dinner, at about eleven.

ROBERT. (*Crosses to* C. *below rostrum. Frantic.*) You can't do that.

BERNARD. Why ever not? There's no rush.

ROBERT. Oh, yes, there is. I assure you you must go at once. Have dinner in the country . . . under the trees . . . surrounded by flowers. It'll be idyllic. (*Crosses* R.)

JACQUELINE. (*Crosses to* L. *of table.*) Yes . . . but I really would prefer to stay here, I'm not home very often.

BERNARD. (*To above table.*) All right, my darling. We'll eat here and then go out to the country at about eleven.

ROBERT. (*Crosses below table to* D. L., *catches* JACQUE-LINE'S *arm as she is about to sit. Shouting.*) You WILL NOT eat here. I insist that you go to the country. . . . You've no idea what it will do for you, the fresh trees and the breath air. (*Starts breathing again.*) Anyway, you're rather pale—

JACQUELINE. Me?

ROBERT. Yes. A little bit pale.

JACQUELINE. (*Crosses* D. R. *above table.*) It's nothing. . . . I'll go and put a fresh face on. (*Goes toward* JUDITH'S *door.*)

ROBERT. (*Runs below table to* D. R. *door to guard it.*) No!

BERNARD. (*Crosses to* R. C.) Look, old man, what on earth is it?

ROBERT. There's no need for her to make up. It's the light—she was standing with the light behind her . . . but now I can see properly. And she's perfect, absolutely perfect as she is.

JACQUELINE. Even so . . . perhaps a little touch of powder.

ROBERT. (*Defending the door.*) Not even a touch, I

forbid it. It might disturb the balance. You are perfect as you are. Lovely!

JACQUELINE. (*To* BERNARD.) Isn't he a darling?

BERNARD. He's a friend. . . . Aren't you, old man?

ROBERT. More than you think.

JACQUELINE. But it's a lady's right to make up her face before dinner.

ROBERT. Yes . . . but you're no lady . . . no, you're different. You are superb, a miracle . . . absolutely perfect as you are. I wouldn't change a whisker.

JACQUELINE. Is that a proposal?

BERNARD. I say, do calm down. (*Breaks* L.)

ROBERT. I am perfectly calm. I am only saying that your fiancée, that Jacqueline, is perfectly all right as she is. And that you will both regret it if you don't go off to dine and spend the night in the country.

BERNARD. (*Sits armchair.*) He's quite right, you know. Well, we'll go for the night, whatever happens . . . at about eleven.

JACQUELINE. (*Crosses, sits* L. *arm of armchair, to* BERNARD.) Well, I'll be perfectly happy to spend the night here. I don't know what's got into you all of a sudden. I thought you loathed the country.

BERNARD. I do. I hate it.

ROBERT. But you're so wrong.

BERNARD. Yes, I know I'm silly about it and that's why I thought we'd go tonight. You don't often get the chance.

ROBERT. Exactly. You mustn't miss this chance!

JACQUELINE. (*Rises, crosses to* ROBERT.) You know, you'll end up by making me think that you don't want me to sleep here tonight.

ROBERT. But how can you say that?

BERNARD. We're only thinking of your good.

ROBERT. (*To* BERNARD.) And yours too, as a matter of fact!

BERNARD. I suppose it might do us both good . . . sleeping with the window open, listening to the wind in the chestnut trees and . . . We'll leave about eleven.

ROBERT. (*Crosses to them; leans across* JACQUELINE *to* BERNARD.) You'll go now and at once. Every second you waste is dangerous and a minute might well be fatal . . . for your health.

BERNARD. You know, old man, it's easy to see that you come from the Provinces. You're so enthusiastic!

ROBERT. I'm doing this all for you, you know. It's nothing to do with me, after all. (*Crosses to* D. R. *door.*)

JACQUELINE. Well, for me, I'm going to fresh up.

ROBERT. (*Backs her away from door.*) You're so nice as you are.

BERNARD. Do leave her alone. Don't you know it's dangerous to argue with women?

ROBERT. Yes.

BERNARD. So why do it?

ROBERT. Look, can't you understand? (*Takes desk chair, puts it in front of* D. C. *door and sits.*)

BERNARD. Understand what?

ROBERT. Look, when I arrived, you said to me, "How are you, old man? It's jolly good to see you." Now you said that, didn't you?

BERNARD. Of course I did, and it's true.

ROBERT. Good. Then you said, "You make yourself at home, fetch your things and when you come back, Robert, you can have that room." (*Points to* JUDITH'S *bedroom.*)

JACQUELINE. Our bedroom?

BERNARD. Did I say that?

ROBERT. You did. You said—it's really my room—

BERNARD. (*Rises.*) No, but wait a minute, what I said was . . .

ROBERT. Bernard!

BERNARD. What I said was . . .

ROBERT. (*Rises, crosses to* BERNARD, *slaps him on* L. *shoulder. Shouts.*) Bernard. (*Returns to* D. R.) Would I lie to you?

BERNARD. No, but you must be confused. (*Puts his arm round* JACQUELINE.) That's our room, Jacqueline's and mine.

ROBERT. But that was the whole point. You said, "You can have our room so you'll feel perfectly at home."

BERNARD. I don't remember.

ROBERT. You'd better remember.

BERNARD. And it's different now. I didn't know that Jacqueline was coming home. So please, I'll have to ask you to give it back.

(BERNARD *and* JACQUELINE *cross toward* D. R. *door.*)

ROBERT. No. (*Stops them.*)

BERNARD. Why not?

ROBERT. I have started to unpack. All my personal things are all over the place. (*Sits chair at* D. R. *door.*) I'd be terribly embarrassed . . .

JACQUELINE. I wouldn't look at them.

ROBERT. That's not the point. I mean, just put yourself in my position. All my little things all over the place . . . and then you, all calm and beautiful, walk in and find chaos.

JACQUELINE. (*Crosses below table to* D. L. *door.* BER-NARD *breaks to* C. ROBERT *replaces chair at desk—to* D. R.) All right . . . all right, if that's how you feel. Really, Bernard, you do choose the most extraordinary friends. (*Takes her Air-France shoulder sack and exits into bedroom 3.*)

BERNARD. (*Crosses to* ROBERT.) Now what on earth's the matter? Are you ill or something?

ROBERT. And Judith? Lufthansa? You'd forgotten all about her I suppose?

BERNARD. Of course not. But she won't be here until after we're gone . . . not till after eleven.

ROBERT. You think so?

BERNARD. Don't you remember? She telephoned saying she was going to be late?

ROBERT. And when you were out she telephoned again to say she was going to be early.

BERNARD. Really? How early?

ROBERT. How early? She's here! (*Points to bedroom.*) She is in there.

BERNARD. (*Rushes to* C. *in panic. Crosses to* ROBERT.) Why didn't you tell me?

ROBERT. (*Leans downstage end of desk.*) Tell you? Where? When? How? In front of Jacqueline? I had ten minutes to try and get you to take her out to dinner. But you, oh no, you decided to economize. . . . You want to eat here!

BERNARD. I didn't understand. . . . I mean, how was I to guess?

ROBERT. You could start by listening to me when I'm talking. (*Crosses below* BERNARD *to his* L.) Really, it's too much. I'm not used to this sort of thing.

BERNARD. (*Crosses* D. R.) Yes. All right. I know you're not.

ROBERT. (*Back to him.*) It's not all right. At least you could thank me for the work I've put in to save you. But no . . . not you. . . . Oh no . . . no! What do you do? You turn on me.

BERNARD. Never.

ROBERT. You did. You turned on me.

BERNARD. Please. Please, Robert. I really didn't understand.

ROBERT. (*Crosses* U. *to door.*) Well, you'd better start trying, because from now you're on your own. I'm finished. I've had enough. I'm going to a hotel . . . and you can just untangle your own harem.

BERNARD. (*Follows him, catches his left arm.*) Please. We must keep calm. We mustn't get worked up. (ROBERT *throws him off.*)

ROBERT. I'm not getting worked up. I'm perfectly calm because I've made up my mind. I'm off . . .

BERNARD. You wouldn't do that. You wouldn't be such a rat.

ROBERT. So I'm a rat. Charming!

BERNARD. No, I didn't mean that.

ROBERT. You did.
BERNARD. I didn't. } (*Business with arms.*)
ROBERT. You did.

(ROBERT *breaks out of* BERNARD'S *attempts to hold them,
third time* ROBERT *exits.* BERNARD *at door.*)

BERNARD. Well, I am sorry. I am frightfully sorry.
ROBERT. (*Enters. Sulks.*) How sorry?
BERNARD. Frightfully.
ROBERT. All right then, I'll stay.
BERNARD. Dear old Robert. I am so grateful to you.
(*They shake hands.* ROBERT *closes door.* BERNARD *crosses*
D. R. *and* ROBERT *follows him to his* L.) This sort of thing
has never happened before.
ROBERT. Now we must keep calm. Whatever happens,
you've got to get Jacqueline out of here, and quickly. I'll
tell Judith that you've been detained somewhere on busi-
ness.
BERNARD. Right. You look after Judith and I'll take
Jacqueline out to Saint Germain. Tomorrow morning she'll
take off and everything will be back to normal.
ROBERT. Well, let's hope she really does take off this
time, because Lufthansa's staying three days.
JUDITH. (*Comes out of the bedroom. She is in her
dressing gown.* ROBERT *rushes to* D. L. *door, bumps back-
wards into door handle.*) Bernard Liebling! You've come
back.
BERNARD. Yes . . . I have . . . I've just come back.
JUDITH. (*Flings her arms round his neck.*) I am so
happy.
BERNARD. So am I. I'm so happy too . . . only I have
got to go out again.
JUDITH. No.
BERNARD. Afraid so.
JUDITH. Then I'll come with you.
BERNARD. Can't be done.
ROBERT. (*Crosses to them.*) Impossible.

JUDITH. But why?

ROBERT. You see, you see, he's got to go out for business reasons.

JUDITH. (*To* ROBERT.) Look, do you mind? Leave us alone for a minute.

BERNARD. You two have met then?

JUDITH. We've met . . . you can go into our room.

ROBERT. My room.

BERNARD. Oh, let him stay . . . he won't be in the way.

JUDITH. He will.

BERNARD. But he's a friend, besides I've got to go out.

BERTHA. (*Enters from kitchen. To* D. C.) Ah. (*Both men in surprise fall on to each other.*) You've come back, sir.

BERNARD. (*Crosses to* R. *of her.*) So it seems.

BERTHA. Miss Judith gave you quite a surprise, I expect.

BERNARD. Yes.

BERTHA. Will you be eating at home, sir?

BERNARD. No, no. I can't make it. But my friend will be eating. Miss Judith, if that's all right, darling?

JUDITH. Without you? (BERTHA *crosses to desk.*)

BERNARD. But I'll be back shortly.

JUDITH. Then I don't want any dinner. (*Crosses to bathroom door* U. L. BERNARD *follows her to* C.) I'll just have a bath and go to bed till you come back.

BERNARD. Please yourself, dear.

JUDITH. I adore you. . . . And did you know that I've got three whole days this time?

BERNARD. That's very good news.

ROBERT. It certainly is very good news.

JUDITH. (*At bathroom. To* ROBERT.) Why are you so pleased?

ROBERT. I'm just happy for you—both of you.

BERNARD. (*Crossing on rostrum.*) Isn't it nice of him? . . . Like being one of the family.

BERTHA. Just like me.

BERNARD. No. Not a bit like you. (*Crosses to* JUDITH. ROBERT *crosses on to rostrum* R. *of* BERNARD.) Now you go and have your bath, my darling. I've got a lot of things to talk over with Robert. . . . Business, you know . . . I'll give you a kiss before I go.

JUDITH. (*Turning back.*) I'll have a little one now please. On account.

BERNARD. Darling, I do think it would be better . . . (ROBERT *slaps* BERNARD—*he falls forward and kisses* JUDITH.)

ROBERT. Do hurry. (BERNARD *kisses and hustles her toward the bathroom.*)

JUDITH. All right, darling. I won't be long. (*Exits into the bathroom just as* JACQUELINE *comes in from the bedroom.* BERNARD, *shaking with fright, sits* U. C. *chair.*)

JACQUELINE. (*At* D. L. *door.*) I knew I was right. . . . I looked an absolute fright.

BERTHA. Oh! But, Miss Jacqueline, I thought . . .

JACQUELINE. I'm not going to take off now until tomorrow.

BERTHA. Tomorrow? But what about . . . (*She gestures toward the bathroom.* BERNARD *slaps down her uplifted arm, which swings back, knocking* ROBERT *into desk chair.* BERNARD *coughs warningly.*)

JACQUELINE. What about what?

BERTHA. I was going to say what about . . .

ROBERT. Think of something else, Bertha.

BERTHA. What about . . . (*Knees sag.*)

ROBERT. That's right. (BERTHA *collapses.* ROBERT *and* BERNARD *catch her—push her hand up and down to revive her.*) I rather think she was going to say, what about a brandy?

BERTHA. (*Crosses below* ROBERT *to drinks on desk, pours a brandy.*) That's it. A brandy.

JACQUELINE. (*To* BERTHA.) Bertha. And you'd better have one yourself. You look as though you've had a shock.

BERNARD. (*Crosses to* JACQUELINE.) Come on, darling, let's go and have dinner.

JACQUELINE. (*Sits* L. *of table.*) But, darling, I've been thinking about it and I want to stay here.

BERNARD. But, darling, it'll be such fun. I need the fresh air.

JACQUELINE. Then you go and get it. Your friend can keep me company.

ROBERT. No! Out of the question.

JACQUELINE. Why is it out of the question?

ROBERT. Because . . . because I've got to go out too. And I've got a terrible headache. (*Sits on* BERTHA's *lap— rises, embarrassed, takes her glass of brandy which she snatches back.*)

JACQUELINE. Well, you'd better go and get some fresh air with Bernard. I'm staying here.

BERNARD. Don't you ever want to do anything but sit at home and slop around in slippers?

JACQUELINE. Look, I travel three hundred thousand miles a year. It's a change to slop around in slippers. I like it. You . . .

BERNARD. I'm only saying . . .

JACQUELINE. Don't interrupt me.

ROBERT. (*Crosses to between armchair and table.*) Think of all that lovely fresh air.

JACQUELINE. We fly at thirty thousand feet, I get enough fresh air. For once I've got a night at home and this is where I'm going to stay.

BERNARD. But . . .

JACQUELINE. (*Rises, crosses below table to* L. *of* BERTHA.) No, I won't listen to another word. I've made up my mind. Bertha, are you feeling better?

(BERNARD *in slightly.* ROBERT *crosses above armchair,* BERNARD *on his* L.)

BERTHA. A little better. It's all this coming and going. It's like the doctor said to my mother, "She's a great tryer but she's not very strong."

JACQUELINE. Do you feel strong enough to cook dinner?

BERTHA. You want to eat here?

ROBERT. No.

JACQUELINE. Yes.

BERNARD. We're going out.

ROBERT. We're all going out.

BERTHA. But you said you were going to eat here.

ROBERT. I've changed my mind.

BERNARD. He's changed his mind. . . .

ROBERT and BERNARD. We've all changed our minds.

JACQUELINE. And I never change my mind. What's for dinner, Bertha?

BERTHA. Sauerkraut and frankfurters.

JACQUELINE. What!

BERTHA. It's nothing to do with me. I don't make up the menus. I just carry out orders.

JACQUELINE. (*To* BERNARD.) Did you ask for frankfurters?

BERNARD. Yes . . . no . . . I don't remember . . . it was Robert.

ROBERT. Me?

BERNARD. Yes. Don't you remember, after you went there—you said you'd never eat anything else.

ROBERT. Went where?

BERNARD. Frankfurt!

ROBERT. Oh yes.

JACQUELINE. (*To* BERTHA.) But haven't you got anything else, Bertha?

BERTHA. I'm afraid not. But it's nice sauerkraut.

JACQUELINE. But I loathe sauerkraut.

ROBERT. (*Quickly.*) So you'd better go out to Saint Germain.

JACQUELINE. (*To* BERTHA.) You're sure you've nothing else?

BERTHA. It's like I was telling the gentlemen. I've defrosted the fridge, you see . . .

JACQUELINE. (*Crosses below table to* D. L. *door.*) All

right, all right . . . you win. We'll go out to Saint Germain. (BERNARD *crosses* L. C.)

ROBERT. You won't regret it.

JACQUELINE. Are you coming with us?

BERNARD. No. He's going to stay here.

JACQUELINE. But you said you were going out.

ROBERT. (*Crosses to above armchair.*) My headache's gone. I'm all lovely.

BERNARD. Yes, he's quite lovely, just look at those roses. Please, Jacqueline, do hurry. I'm absolutely starving.

JACQUELINE. I'll get my handbag. (*Exits into bedroom D. L.*)

BERNARD. The timetables are up the creek, old boy.

ROBERT. Take it easy, Bernard, we're nearly there. Just hang on for a little longer.

JUDITH. (*Enters from the bathroom, crosses onto* R. *of rostrum.*) There we are then. I wasn't long, was I?

ROBERT. Do keep your voice down.

JUDITH. What?

ROBERT. (*Pointing to* BERNARD.) He's got a headache.

BERNARD. (*Breaks to* ROBERT's *left.*) I feel terrible.

JUDITH. (*Crosses to* BERNARD.) My poor darling . . . I'll get you an aspirin.

BERTHA. Get two for me too.

JUDITH. (*Crosses below the men, heading toward bedroom.*) It'll clear up in no time.

BERNARD. (*Frantic.*) No. No.

ROBERT. (*Stops* JUDITH.) No—no. I know, what about a bath?

BERNARD. She's just had one, you fool.

ROBERT. (*Brings* JUDITH *between them.*) Have another.

JUDITH. I've not had one yet. The water's too hot.

ROBERT. Well, go and try it again—before it gets too cold.

BERNARD. (*Pushing her off to* U. L.) Yes, it gets cold very quickly.

JUDITH. You won't go away?

BERNARD. (*At bathroom.*) No, no . . . later. . . . (*Pushes her into the bathroom just as* JACQUELINE *enters from the bedroom.* BERNARD *shuts the door. Crossing to* L. C. *on* JACQUELINE'S *entrance.*) Later . . . we're going to the country.

BERTHA. (*Crossing to* BERNARD *and giving him a brandy.*) Here. (BERNARD *chokes over his drink. To* ROBERT.) Do you want one? (*Crosses to* R.)

ROBERT. Not if it's going to do what it did to him— Yes, I'd better have one, Bertha.

JACQUELINE. Don't you feel very well now?

ROBERT. I feel like an airplane. My head's going round like a propeller.

BERTHA. (*Hands* ROBERT *a drink.*) I expect we're in for a thunderstorm.

ROBERT. That'll be nice.

JACQUELINE. (*Starts to sit* L. *of table.*) Well, if there's going to be a storm, it'd be silly to go out.

BERNARD. (*Grabs her and crosses* U.) Oh, but you haven't lived until you have seen a storm in the country.

JACQUELINE. All right. See you later. (*Exits front door.* ROBERT *slams main door in* BERNARD'S *face to stop him.*)

ROBERT. (R. *on rostrum.*) And for heaven's sake keep her at Saint Germain.

BERNARD. (*To him—hands him his glass.*) Don't worry. She gets back here over my dead body. But you'll stay here? You can't leave me now.

ROBERT. I couldn't if I wanted to. I haven't got the strength. Enjoy yourself.

JACQUELINE. (*Entering front door.*) If you don't hurry, darling—I won't go. (*Exits as* JUDITH *enters from the bathroom.* BERNARD *slams front door, leans on it.* ROBERT, *in panic, dashes through swing door of kitchen, re-entering at once.*)

JUDITH. It's still too hot.

BERNARD. What is?

JUDITH. The water.

BERNARD. Well, blow on it.

JUDITH. You're going now?

BERNARD. (*Opens door, blocking his view of* ROBERT *who has sat on chair behind it.*) Yes, darling, I'm going right now. But Robert's here. Robert . . . Robert. (*Discovers* ROBERT *and exits.* BERNARD *exits as* JUDITH *goes back into the bathroom.*)

ROBERT. Ouf! (*Drinks from both glasses, rises, crosses down—sits in armchair.*)

BERTHA. Well done, sir. I'd go a long way to see something like that again. You played it like a champion. . . . Cheers . . . and congratulations. (*Pours a drink for him.*)

ROBERT. And that one too, please, Bertha. (*Holding out second glass.*)

BERTHA. It was pretty close.

ROBERT. It was a photo finish.

(The TELEPHONE RINGS. ROBERT *jumps.* BERTHA *answers it.)*

BERTHA. (*At phone.*) Hello. Yes, I'll take it. A message from a Miss Janet Hawkins? "Storm over Gander and the North Atlantic Stop will be back in Paris at twenty-two hours G.M.T." . . . What does G.M.T. mean? None of my business? . . . Right. (*Hangs up.*) You heard all that?

ROBERT. (*Weak.*) Every word, Bertha. (BERTHA *gives him another drink.*)

BERTHA. (R. *of him.*) Here . . . you'd better have another one of these. Because if you ask me it's out with the cigarettes and on with the safety belts. . . . If I read the signs right, Mr. Robert, I'd say we're in for a happy night! (*Raises her glass.* ROBERT *groans.*)

CURTAIN

END OF ACT ONE

ACT TWO

JUDITH, *followed by* ROBERT, *enters from the dining room.*

JUDITH. (*Crosses to above table.*) If you really want to annoy me by being rude about German food . . .

ROBERT. (*Following.*) I'm not being rude about anything.

BERTHA. (*Enters from kitchen door.*) Will you want any coffee?

JUDITH. Not for me, Bertha, you know it keeps me awake.

BERTHA. How about you, sir?

ROBERT. I'd better have some . . . otherwise that sauerkraut will give me nightmares.

BERTHA. All right.

JUDITH. I can tell you, you're wasting your time if you think you can annoy me by being rude about German food.

ROBERT. I'm not being rude about anything. I just find that pickled cabbage weighs me down a bit.

JUDITH. Nobody seems to get nightmares in Germany.

ROBERT. I expect you're used to it. It's a question of heredity.

JUDITH. They eat sauerkraut in other places, you know.

ROBERT. Bully for them. (*Breaks* R.) All I said was it's heavy . . . very heavy.

JUDITH. (*To him.*) When it's nicely prepared and served with chilled wine like we had it tonight—it's delicious.

ROBERT. But heavy, delicious—but heavy. My cheeks are burning, aren't yours?

JUDITH. (*Breaks* L.) No.

ROBERT. (*Crosses to above armchair.*) Anyway, let's not quarrel about it.

JUDITH. (*To* D. L.) What else is there to do?

ROBERT. Let's go out.

JUDITH. (*Shocked.*) Together?

ROBERT. Now do relax. It's not an order, you know—only a suggestion.

BERTHA. (*Enters* R. *of armchair to below table, puts tray down and crosses between table and armchair—crosses toward kitchen door.*) Here we are, sir. And if I were you, sir, I'd drink it while it's hot because . . . (*Gestures at his stomach. Back to rostrum.*)

ROBERT. You may be right.

JUDITH. (*Crosses below to desk chair.*) Bertha! When did Mr. Bernard say he'd be back?

BERTHA. (*To her.*) Well, it's difficult to say. . . .

ROBERT. He's out on business.

JUDITH. I wasn't asking you. I was talking to Bertha.

BERTHA. Well, I don't know much more than he does. Mr. Bernard went out, and of course I know when he went out. But I won't know when he'll be back until he does get back.

(ROBERT *above table, about to pour out coffee* [*does not do so*].)

JUDITH. Thank you, Berta.

BERTHA. I mean, he doesn't tell me everything.

JUDITH. Well, he could have told me.

BERTHA. Yes, of course and he would have done. But it all happened so suddenly . . . something unforeseen. Isn't that so, sir?

ROBERT. (*Crosses to* BERTHA.) Yes. That's how the unforeseen happens . . . it's something one just doesn't foresee.

BERTHA. Of course not, as it's unforeseen . . . you see.

ROBERT. Exactly. Because if we'd been able to foresee it, it wouldn't have been unforeseen. It would have been . . . What would it have been, Bertha?

BERTHA. Something quite different. You see.

ROBERT. Something quite different.

BERTHA. You see.

JUDITH. Yes. Thank you, Bertha. I do see.

BERTHA. You're quite welcome, Miss Judith. (*Exits to kitchen.*)

ROBERT. (*To* JUDITH.) If I hadn't had that sauerkraut, do you know I would have enjoyed myself very much.

JUDITH. Why?

ROBERT. Well, Bernard wasn't here, and it was very nice—just the two of us. So come on, just try and smile a little just for me. You're really very, very pretty for . . . for . . .

JUDITH. (*Breaks* R.) For a German, I suppose?

ROBERT. (*Crosses to armchair and sits.*) I do wish we could keep politics out of it.

JUDITH. Politics! You're the one who's been trying all the little subtle tricks . . . a wink here . . . a little secret smile there . . . you didn't once stop grinning at me all through the meal.

ROBERT. I can't help it if I think you're rather nice.

JUDITH. You think what you like. I think you're a bit of a . . .

ROBERT. No, I'm not—I'm not really. Why don't we go for a little drive in the country?

JUDITH. At this time of night?

ROBERT. It's not late.

JUDITH. It may not be late but it's dark. We wouldn't see a thing.

ROBERT. Who wants to see? It's just an idea to repay your hospitality. We can get some fresh air, have a little walk . . . and I'll be awfully good. I won't try anything . . . word of honor!

JUDITH. (*Sarcastic.*) Oh yes! Word of honor!

ROBERT. There's no risk, really there isn't. I mean, you're big enough—well, capable enough—to defend yourself, if you really think I'd try to take advantage of you.

JUDITH. I refuse to listen to that sort of thing!

ROBERT. (*Rises to her.*) But you're so charming . . . and anyway it's only a game.

JUDITH. A dangerous game.

ROBERT. Nonsense! How could it be dangerous? You've got Bernard.

JUDITH. All right. So I've got Bernard. But even if it's not dangerous, in the first place it doesn't appeal to me, and in the second, I think it's dishonest.

ROBERT. (*Turns away.*) When you kissed me . . .

JUDITH. By mistake!

ROBERT. (*Crosses and sits on arm of armchair.*) Maybe. But you did kiss me a second time.

JUDITH. The first time was purely accidental and the second time was to keep you quiet.

ROBERT. (*Doubling up with pain.*) *Please,* Judith.

JUDITH. Is it a sort of obsession?

ROBERT. No, I think it's wind. Oh yes, I'd call it a romantic obsession.

JUDITH. Romantic! I must say you look romantic— sitting there all red and congested!

ROBERT. That's because of the wine—and because I really do need some fresh air.

JUDITH. (*Crosses to him.*) Well, as long as we're not too late.

ROBERT. (*Rises.*) Oh! You *are* a darling. (*Hugs her.*)

JUDITH. (*Furious; backing away.*) Put me down . . . word of honor indeed. My mother warned me about men like you!

ROBERT. Please . . . I got carried away. I was just pleased that you agreed with me for once.

JUDITH. Yes. When we were out in the country, in the dark, and in your car, I suppose you'd get carried away again. (*Crosses D. L.*) You'd pounce on me!

ROBERT. Pounce on you in my car. Impossible! I haven't got a car. We would have to take a taxi and the driver would chaperone us. I could say to the driver the lady's rather nervous so would you please mind coming and sitting in the back.

JUDITH. (*Crosses to above chair* L.) No, I'm not going.
ROBERT. Please. . . .

JUDITH. No, I've had enough. You come in here like some dreadful vandal, think up all sorts of devilish plots, try and get me away from my fiancé and up some pitch-black country lane . . . You want me to go out! Right! I'm going! But on my own!

ROBERT. (*Stopping her.*) Listen . . . liebchen!

JUDITH. Don't you liebchen me. How dare you be so familiar! I will *not* listen! Not another word . . . you're not a . . .

BERTHA. (*Enters from kitchen.*) Do you want some more coffee?

ROBERT. No, no, of course not. We haven't touched this yet. (BERTHA *peering round kitchen door.* ROBERT *motions her to go.*) Judith, please listen to me.

JUDITH. (*Crossing to* D. R. *door.*) I will not listen to you. I shall never listen to you again—you vandal! (*Exits slamming the door.*)

BERTHA. (*At door.*) She's a bit upset?

ROBERT. Yes . . . but very charming.

BERTHA. (D.) Won't she go out with you?

ROBERT. (*Sits armchair.*) No, unfortunately.

BERTHA. (*Crosses* D. R. C.) Well, I'm afraid you'll have to cope with the American then.

ROBERT. Cope with an . . . Are you out of your mind? This is my first day in Paris and I've had just about enough of you, Mr. Bernard, and especially that sauerkraut—it's rumbling.

JANET. (*Enters* U. C. ROBERT *rises to* D. R.) Hi!

BERTHA. (*To* R. *of her.*) Ah, good evening, Miss Janet.

JANET. There was a terrible storm over the North Atlantic and we had to turn back. . . . Isn't it marvelous! Another whole night at home! Where's Bernard?

ROBERT. He's just gone out.

BERTHA. Yes . . . on business.

JANET. Not for long, I hope.

BERTHA. Oh no, not for long.

JANET. (*Crossing to desk, puts bag on chair. To* ROBERT.) Fine. And how have you got on since I left this morning?

(BERTHA *crosses to* R. C.)

ROBERT. (*Crosses to* D. R. *door.*) It's been quite a little day.

JANET. Isn't it cozy here?

ROBERT. It's going to get cozier.

JANET. I adore coming home. Everything's so calm here.

ROBERT. Yes. Quite uneventful, in fact.

JANET. (*Puts down her bag—which is labeled T.W.A. —on a chair and goes toward the bedroom.*) Excuse me.

ROBERT. Where are you going?

JANET. I want to get out of this uniform.

ROBERT. The other room!

JANET. What?

ROBERT. Use the other room.

JANET. Why?

ROBERT. To get out of your uniform.

JANET. But my room—Bernard's and mine—is that one.

ROBERT. I know, but I'm in it now. He told me to take it. "You're my best friend," he said, "so you have my room while Janet's in America, it's the nicest room in the flat."

JANET. I see. . . .

BERTHA. He's right, you know. That's what Mr. Bernard said.

ROBERT. So I unpacked my bags.

JANET. Well, pack them again and move them over there.

ROBERT. Impossible.

BERTHA. Out of the question.

JANET. For heaven's sake! But it's not all that difficult!

ROBERT. It is! I think we ought to wait until Bernard gets back.

BERTHA. Yes. He gave the orders. It wouldn't do to cross him.

JANET. Just a minute! Who's in charge here? Bernard or me?

ROBERT and BERTHA. Mr. Bernard.

JANET. Yes, but I happen to be the mistress in this house.

ROBERT. No comment.

JANET. And in America, the mistress of the house gives the orders. And the man obeys without arguing. The man makes the money and the woman does the thinking . . . so out of the way!

ROBERT. Just a minute . . . we happen to be in France, and in France, it's the master who gives the orders . . . I'm very sorry but that's the way it is.

JANET. (*Crosses to above table and pours coffee.*) Look, I'm too tired and hungry to make a song and dance about it, but as soon as I've had a coffee and something to eat you and I are going to have a little talk. And I'll lay you fifty dollars to one of your new francs that you're going to agree with me before you're very much older.

ROBERT. (R. *of* BERTHA.) I'm at your service.

JANET. What have you got to eat, Bertha?

BERTHA. There's some frankfurters.

ROBERT. (*Crosses to desk.*) And sauerkraut.

JANET. Any fresh cream?

BERTHA. For dessert?

JANET. No. To have with the frankfurters and sauerkraut.

(ROBERT *flops on desk in disgust, takes a drink—sits desk chair.*)

BERTHA. (*Bewildered.*) Like the molasses on the pancakes.

JANET. Yes. And bring the molasses as well.

BERTHA. (*Crossing to kitchen.*) Well, you're a grown woman. And an American. I suppose you know what agrees with you . . . you'd better come into the kitchen and eat it. It wouldn't look right in here. (*Goes off, muttering, into the kitchen.* JANET *follows with coffee.*)

JANET. And do you have any of those little gherkins? I'm crazy for gherkins. (*Exits just as* JUDITH *enters— in uniform—from* D. R. *bedroom, with bag.*)

JUDITH. See you later?

ROBERT. (*Rises.*) Where are you going?

JUDITH. Out.

ROBERT. What am I going to say to Bernard? He told me to look after you.

JUDITH. Well, you've certainly gone about it in a very peculiar way. All that winking and grinning! And you've got a very funny look in those wicked blue eyes of yours.

ROBERT. Blue? But they're not blue! They're azure. On my passport it says "eyes azure." Look . . . come closer . . . come and look at them.

JUDITH. No, thank you. (ROBERT *crosses to* L. *of armchair.*) I can see well enough from here— (*As* JUDITH *crosses* R. *to the front door she sees the T.W.A. bag on desk chair.*) —and it's safer that way. (D. *slightly.*) Whose is this? This T.W.A. bag.

ROBERT. (*To her. Seizing it.*) It's mine.

JUDITH. What do you want with a handbag?

ROBERT. Well, I keep my little things in it . . .

JUDITH. Ah, if you were patriotic, you'd keep your little things in an Air-France bag.

ROBERT. I never thought of that.

JUDITH. (*Crossing to front door.*) You're all the same. Insensitive, unthinking, and unpatriotic! (*Exits through the front door just as* JANET *returns, eating a sandwich. On* JUDITH's *exit,* ROBERT *is between armchair and desk, tries to open catch of bag.*)

JANET. (*Crosses to* L. *of* ROBERT.) What are you looking for!

ROBERT. Me? (*Caught by surprise—loses hold of bag, catches it in mid-air.*)

JANET. Yes, you.

ROBERT. What an extraordinary thing to ask.

JANET. You happen to be clutching my bag.

ROBERT. Me? (*Understanding at last.*) Oh, excuse me. (*Still hangs on to the bag.*)

JANET. There's no money in it. I pay everything by check.

ROBERT. But you're so wise. I mean, it's much easier that way.

JANET. There's a Parker pen, a lipstick, and a few little personal things for the night, that's all. . . . You can believe me.

ROBERT. But of course I believe you.

JANET. Well, put it down then.

ROBERT. What? Oh, I see. (*Puts it down.*) Do forgive me, it was purely mechanical . . . you left it on the chair. I came along and I wanted to sit down. I didn't want to sit on it so I picked it up—it was mechanical—a sort of mechanical clutch.

JANET. (*Sniffs. Takes her bag and stalks off toward the bedroom,* D. R. *Sarcastic.*) I suppose I'm allowed in here!

ROBERT. Certainly . . . make yourself at home. (*Sits desk chair.*)

JANET. Thank you. . . . I happen to be at home. (*Exits, slamming the door.* ROBERT *mops his brow, but* JANET *returns almost at once—holding the Lufthansa handbag. Aggressive.*) Whose is this? (*Re-enters.*) This Lufthansa bag?

ROBERT. It's mine! It's mine! (*Snatches bag—crosses* L.)

JANET. What do you want with a handbag?

ROBERT. (*Crosses to* JANET.) I keep my little things for the night in it . . . my pajamas . . . my toothbrush . . . spare pair of socks.

JANET. (*Crosses below* ROBERT *to his* L.) You don't have to make an inventory. But I'd rather you used one of our T.W.A. ones—not that I'm anti-German or anything—but they're much more practical. Ours have a

little pocket inside—with a zip fastener. This one doesn't.
. . . Look. (*Begins to open it.* ROBERT *snatches it away.*)

ROBERT. No. No, mine has plenty of pockets. Hundreds.
I have got lots of tiny, tiny pockets.

JANET. I'd still like to make you a present of one of
ours.

ROBERT. That's very kind of you.

JANET. (*Crosses* L. C. *Puts her own bag on table.*)
More than you know. It's not very often that American
women give presents. But you refused to let me into my
own room and, do you know, I rather admire that.

ROBERT. You do?

JANET. (*Sits back of armchair.*) It's not often we come
across that sort of hostility. Mind you, it's just as well.
We want America to stay a great country.

ROBERT. I don't quite understand.

JANET. Do you know why America is a great country?

ROBERT. (D. *slightly.*) Well . . . it's a big . . . very
big . . . they have tremendous resources?—no? Their
resources are quite untapped?

JANET. No. It's very simple. It's because American men
never grow up.

ROBERT. Never?

JANET. The Kinsey report proved it.

ROBERT. Did it?

JANET. We women are much stronger, because our hus-
bands always agree with us. They have to.

ROBERT. And they don't mind?

JANET. Oh. Of course they mind. But one little mutiny
and we're off to Reno. (*Rises, crosses to* ROBERT D. R.)
You can get a divorce there in six weeks—for mental
cruelty. And that means alimony.

ROBERT. What happens if they don't pay?

JANET. Jail.

ROBERT. Jail!

JANET. So to avoid going to jail they pay up, and to
pay up, they have to work. This ensures a stable economy.
So we're a great country.

ROBERT. (*Crosses to armchair and sits.*) Poor old Bernard!

JANET. Why?

ROBERT. You're going to marry him, aren't you?

JANET. Never.

ROBERT. Why not?

JANET. (*Leans on R. back of armchair.*) He's a Frenchman. He's grown up. He might argue with me . . . and I couldn't take that. I shall just have to marry an American. But I shall always love Bernard.

ROBERT. So you'll marry an American but you won't necessarily love him?

JANET. (*Breaks down slightly.*) How could I? How can you love a man who spends his whole time working?

ROBERT. It's not impossible.

JANET. Oh! Do say that again.

ROBERT. What?

JANET. "It's not impossible."

ROBERT. Why?

JANET. Your lips make such a pretty shape when you say it.

ROBERT. (*Flattered.*) Really?

JANET. Truly . . . say it again.

ROBERT. Say what again?

JANET. "It's not impossible."

ROBERT. (*Sky.*) It's not impossible.

JANET. There they go! . . . all little! Do it again.

ROBERT. Again?

JANET. Please . . . for me.

ROBERT. It's not possible.

JANET. Like a little flower.

ROBERT. You embarrass me.

JANET. No . . . no. . . . Say, have you ever kissed an American?

ROBERT. Me?

JANET. Yes.

ROBERT. No, I'm afraid not. The opportunity has never presented itself.

JANET. (*Brings desk chair to* R. *of* ROBERT *and sits.*) Now that's a great shame. We're like the French really— very rational about love.

ROBERT. Really?

JANET. I'll show you. (*Pulling him by his lapels up to her, she kisses him.*) How was that?

ROBERT. I'm afraid I'm not expert.

JANET. That's why it's interesting.

ROBERT. Yes. But I find it very difficult to give an opinion. You see, I've never kissed anyone before without having some sort of reason.

JANET. I only want to know what you think of my technique.

ROBERT. It's come as bit of a surprise . . . I wasn't expecting it.

JANET. No, I suppose you weren't.

ROBERT. You just want my opinion.

JANET. Yes. Just your opinion. So let's try again. . . . Ready?

ROBERT. (*Polite.*) After you.

(*She pushes him back in armchair. They kiss again, and during the embrace the DOORBELL RINGS.*)

JANET. How was that one?

ROBERT. Could you give me a lift up? I was concentrating that time. It was certainly better than the first.

JANET. Yes, but how was it—technically?

ROBERT. There was a distinct ringing in my ears.

JANET. That's good.

ROBERT. Oh, that's good, is it?

JANET. That's very good. So let's try it again.

(*They embrace a third time. The DOORBELL sounds again and* BERTHA *enters to answer it. She exits.*)

ROBERT. Now that was really very impressive. The ringing sound was much louder. Congratulations.

JANET. You're welcome. It's always interesting. Especially when you find someone with a cute little mouth like yours. . . . Say it again.

ROBERT. I can't go on saying it.

JANET. Please. Pretty please, for me. What are you doing? (ROBERT *has turned his face away from her.*)

ROBERT. Just having a dummy run. It's NOT impossible.

JANET. I can't resist it.

ROBERT. I can see that.

JANET. I must! Come on! (*Seizes his lapels.*)

ROBERT. No, can't you see all this technique will end up giving me ideas?

JANET. Now, Robert, but you mustn't get any ideas. The technique of the kiss is based on not having any ideas.

ROBERT. Not having any ideas?

JANET. No.

ROBERT. But what's the point of it then?

JANET. It helps to pass the time.

ROBERT. It helps to pass the time?

JANET. I mean, when you're with people you don't much care for—well, you can't play gin-rummy all the time, can you?

ROBERT. I can't play it at all.

JANET. So when you meet someone with such a cute little mouth like yours—well, it's a good chance to get in some practice. . . . Shall we? (*Digs him with a forefinger, he starts to do likewise.*)

ROBERT. Help yourself. (*She kisses him, just as* BERNARD *enters.*)

(BERTHA *follows* BERNARD *on, closes front door, and exits through kitchen.*)

BERNARD. (*Crosses to desk, picks up timetable.*) What with one thing and another I'd forgotten my keys. (*He sees* JANET.) Hello, darling— Bertha told me you'd come back.

JANET. Your friend was keeping me company.

BERNARD. Oughtn't you to be in New York, darling?

JANET. I know, sweetie. But I telephoned to tell you about the storm—

BERNARD. Storm! (*Throws timetable into wastepaper basket.*) Ah well.

JANET. And you were out. Where were you?

BERNARD. On business.

JANET. You look worried about something.

BERNARD. Worried? I'm not worried. (*Sees* ROBERT *silently mouthing. To* ROBERT.) Everything all right, old man?

ROBERT. It's not impossible. . . . I mean, splendid!

BERNARD. No hitches?

ROBERT. Not for the moment—no.

JANET. Your friend and I were having a fascinating . . .

ROBERT. Chat. Till you got back, old boy.

BERNARD. Well, I'm back now.

ROBERT. Lovely to see you.

BERNARD. And I'm going to interrupt your conversation to take you out for the night to Saint Germain.

JANET. Why?

BERNARD. A sudden inspiration.

ROBERT. (*Rises, leaving bag on floor below armchair, crosses to* U. L.) An absolutely marvelous inspiration.

BERNARD. It'll make a change for you.

JANET. (*Rises.*) It's awfully sweet of you, darling, but I'm much too tired.

BERNARD. Come on, dear.

JANET. Let's stay here. I'll just have a bath and then we can go to bed. And we'll have enough change as it is, you've given our room to your friend.

BERNARD. Darling, do listen!

JANET. I know, let's try this room over here. (*Rises, picks up her own bag from table—crosses to* U. L. *bedroom.*)

ROBERT. (*Crosses to* L. *of her.*) No!

JANET. Why not?

BERNARD. (*Crosses to* C. *stage.*) Yes. Why not?

ROBERT. You told Bertha she could sleep in this one.

BERNARD. That's right.

JANET. Ins'ead of sleeping in her own room? Why?

ROBERT. That's the whole point. It's perfectly reasonable, after all. You're traveling all the time. Well, Bertha gets a little jealous . . . she decides she wants to travel too across the flat.

JANET. (*To* BERNARD.) Where would you have slept if I hadn't come?

BERNARD. (*At a gesture from* ROBERT.) Me? Well . . . over there . . . in that one.

BERTHA. (*Enters to* C. *on rostrum.* BERNARD *crosses* R. *to desk.*) Is that all for tonight then?

JANET. (*Crosses to* BERTHA—D. *of rostrum.*) Bertha, is the bed made up in there?

BERTHA. No.

JANET. (*Crosses to* BERTHA.) No. Well, if Mr. Bernard's friend has our room, where are we going to sleep?

BERTHA. Oh! He's got your room, has he? Well then . . . (*Sees* ROBERT *pointing* D. L., *does likewise.*) . . . over there I suppose.

JANET. You don't imagine we're all going to tuck in with you, Bertha?

BERTHA. Me?

ROBERT. You must remember, Bertha. You said you wanted a change.

BERTHA. I did?

ROBERT. You wanted to get a change of scenery.

BERTHA. Me?

ROBERT. Yes. I heard you.

BERNARD. Is that clear?

BERTHA. No.

JANET. (*Takes* BERTHA's *hand and exits bedroom* U. L. *with her.*) Come on, blue-eyes. I'll give you a hand. I can't understand a word those boys are babbling about.

BERTHA. I could do with some help. (*They exit.*)

BERNARD. (*Crosses to* ROBERT.) Where is she?

JANET. Who?

BERNARD. Jacqueline.

ROBERT. How should I know? You were taking her out to Saint Germain.

BERNARD. We never got there. We had a tiff in the restaurant, in the middle of the meal she upped and walked out on me. By the time I got into the street she'd vanished.

ROBERT. And Judith went out for a walk.

BERNARD. Well, that's all right then. Now all I've got to do is get Janet out to Saint Germain until tomorrow morning.

ROBERT. You want to watch it. You're getting a complex about the country.

BERNARD. Can't be helped. If Jacqueline comes back I can't be here and you mustn't know anything.

ROBERT. What if Judith gets back?

BERNARD. Let's worry about that if and when it happens.

ROBERT. That's all right for you. But I'm the one who'll have to do all the talking.

BERNARD. I'm sorry . . . but my nerves, you know, they're beginning to let me down. How are yours?

ROBERT. Bearing up. It's a great change after Aix. But I'll admit it's interesting, even exciting.

JANET. (*Returns with* BERTHA. JANET *remains by door* U. L. BERTHA *crosses above her to kitchen door.*) It's a darling room! Much better than the country.

BERNARD. (*Crosses below* ROBERT *to* JANET. *Weak.*) . . . The chestnut trees . . . the wind. (*A DOOR SLAMS offstage.*) What was that?

ROBERT. The wind.

BERTHA. The front door.

BERNARD. (*He suddenly wakes up, pushes* JANET *into* U. L. *bedroom.*) I've just realized, I've never seen inside that room. (*Whispers, "All yours, old man," to* ROBERT.)

ROBERT. I say—you can't do this. . . . (ROBERT *then vanishes after* JANET *just as* JACQUELINE *enters.*)

BERTHA. (*To* ROBERT.) It's like I was saying, sir. . . . (*Exits kitchen on* JACQUELINE'S *entrance.*)

JACQUELINE. (*To* ROBERT.) Where is he?

ROBERT. (*Hides under standard lamp* U. L.) Who? (*Reappears.*)

JACQUELINE. Bernard.

ROBERT. I thought he was with you. At Saint Germain.

JACQUELINE. Look, what's going on? (*Bangs front door—crosses off rostrum to* C.) All through the journey, all throught the meal, all Bernard could do was babble about fresh air and chestnut trees. He went on and on just as if he was trying to hide something.

ROBERT. What would he want to hide?

JACQUELINE. Well, I know he's got nothing to hide. I know him too well. But all this pastoral stuff is getting me down. (*Wanders toward the main bedroom* D. R.)

ROBERT. (*Following her.*) That's my room.

JACQUELINE. What?

ROBERT. My room.

JACQUELINE. Oh, of course, I'm sorry. I don't know where I am.

ROBERT. Who does?

JACQUELINE. I'm quite worn out. I mean I just went out to get some air and when I came back into the restaurant, he'd gone.

ROBERT. Well, perhaps he went out to get some air. And perhaps after you left he went back. So perhaps he's upset too. He loves you, you know.

JACQUELINE. I know he loves me and I love him. I expect none of this would happen if only we could be together all the time. When he's here all alone and I'm at the other side of the world, well, I often wonder what he's up to. It upsets me.

ROBERT. And it's the same for him. It upsets him. (*Looking at the door through which* BERNARD *and* JANET *have just exited.*) That's why he probably wanted to spend a few hours in the country so you could discuss all this.

JACQUELINE. It would all be so simple if only we could get married.

ROBERT. That might solve everything . . . well, nearly everything.

JACQUELINE. I mean it's really too stupid to spend all that time apart.

ROBERT. Stupid.

JACQUELINE. (*Below armchair—picks up handbag in* R. *hand and turns, starts to cross* L.) Never mind, when we're married it'll all be lovely. (*Finds the Lufthansa handbag.*) Whose is this? This Lufthansa bag?

ROBERT. (*Taking bag. Shouting.*) It's mine! It's MINE! I use it to keep little things for the night in . . . my pajamas, socks, spare pair of toothbrushes . . .

JACQUELINE. How extraordinary.

ROBERT. It's not illegal, is it?

JACQUELINE. . . . . I suppose it's all right. (*Looks at him with some suspicion.*) Anyway I'm too tired to start arguing. (*Crosses to bedroom* D. L.) I'm going to bed. And when Bernard gets back you can tell him to come in and apologize to me . . . and tell him he's made me very unhappy.

ROBERT. All right, Jacqueline.

JACQUELINE. Thank you, Robert. . . . Good night.

ROBERT. Good night.

(JACQUELINE *exits into the second bedroom.* ROBERT *throws bag into bedroom* D. R., *slams door.* BERNARD *and* JANET *enter from the bedroom.* JANET *is wearing her dressing gown and carrying her bath cap.*)

JANET. Now for heaven's sake, stop bullying me. I don't want to go to Saint Germain-en-Laye. I'm perfectly happy here. Robert, you tell him.

ROBERT. Well . . . it's difficult . . . please don't ask me.

BERNARD. (C.) Darling, it'll be such fun. You'll love it.

JANET. And I adore that little bedroom . . . and now I'm going to take a bath. (*She exits into bathroom.*)

BERNARD. (*Above armchair.*) Which one was it?

ROBERT. Jacqueline.

BERNARD. Where?

ROBERT. There . . . no, there. (*Pointing to* D. L. *room.*)

BERNARD. (*Crosses to table.*) What on earth am I going to do? (*Cools forehead with heavy glass ashtray.*) I can't take much more of this.

ROBERT. (*Crosses to* BERNARD'S R.) Just take it easy, Bernard. Remember that Judith will probably be back in a minute. So whatever we do you mustn't panic. (*Enter* JACQUELINE *from* D. L. *bedroom.*) There's Jacqueline.

JACQUELINE. (*Remains by* D. L. *door.* ROBERT *crosses onto rostrum to bathroom door. To* BERNARD.) So you've come back, have you? How dare you?

BERNARD. Come back?

JACQUELINE. After leaving me in the middle of dinner.

BERNARD. But you left me.

JACQUELINE. I went back into the restaurant and you'd gone.

BERNARD. Now just because we all got a little hysterical . . .

JACQUELINE. We got hysterical? You got hysterical! It's not enough to have a place of our own, a flat like this. We have to go tramping off into the country to sleep, just as though we were trying to hide from something.

BERNARD. Shush!

JACQUELINE. (*Forte.*) Don't you shush me.

ROBERT. (*Breaks down and back to bathroom door.*) Shush!

JACQUELINE. Nor you. I don't want to go into hiding. You do, I suppose. Because you're ashamed of not marrying me.

BERNARD. But of course I'll marry you if I really want me to—you're my fiancée.

JACQUELINE. I'm your mistress. That's why you go around shushing me. Mistresses are always shushed.

BERNARD. Jacqueline, please . . . not in front of Robert.

JACQUELINE. Why not? He's your friend, he's probably on your side.

ROBERT. (*Breaks down and back to bathroom door.*) Please . . . pretend I'm not here . . . I've no experience of love and all that.

JACQUELINE. (*Backs* BERNARD *across stage to desk.*) That's it. That's the very word! Love! We ought to be proud of it. Tell everybody about it! Tell the whole world.

BERNARD. I agree. I absolutely agree . . . but please, Jacqueline . . . not so loud.

ROBERT. Bernard. Not so loud. Do keep calm, Jacqueline.

JACQUELINE. (*Moves to bathroom door, stopped at* C. *rostrum.*) All right. I'll try . . . I know, I'll have a bath.

BERNARD. (*To* D. *of bathroom door, defending the door.*) No, no . . . you can't.

JACQUELINE. Why not?

BERNARD. (*Points to* ROBERT.) He's going to have one.

ROBERT. Am I? (*Slow, bewildered cross to door.*)

BERNARD. Yes.

JACQUELINE. Surely he can have one after me.

ROBERT. Superstitious . . . very unlucky.

JACQUELINE. Really!

BERNARD. He's our guest. He said it's unlucky.

JACQUELINE. But surely he can let me go first.

ROBERT. No. Everybody's got to wait their turn in the queue. (*Both* MEN *turn upstage to form a queue.*)

JACQUELINE. (*Crosses to* D. L.) Well, I must say your friend is terribly considerate. A gentleman, quite over-poweringly polite. . . .

BERNARD. Jacqueline, darling . . .

JACQUELINE. And you stand there and let him insult me! (BERNARD *on* ROBERT'S R.)

ROBERT and BERNARD. (*To above table.*) SHUSH!

(JACQUELINE *marches into the* D. L. *bedroom and slams the door behind her, just as* JANET *enters from the bathroom.*)

JANET. (*To* L. *chair.*) I really do feel much better.
ROBERT. Shush!
JANET. (*Sotto voce.*) I really do feel much better.
ROBERT. Well, I'm glad someone does.
JANET. (*To* BERNARD.) Coming, darling?
BERNARD. In a minute, darling.
ROBERT. Yes. In a minute, darling. . . . I'll be right in. (*Sits* L. *arm of armchair.*)
JANET. Don't be too long. I've had a very tiring day.
BERNARD. Me too.
ROBERT. And it's not over yet.
JANET. Have you much more to do?
BERNARD. (*Breaks to* C.) Just a few things to clear up.
JANET. Good. . . . Don't be too long. Good night. (*Kisses* BERNARD.) Good night, Robert dear. No, please don't get up— Good night. (*Goes into the third bedroom.*)
ROBERT. (*Rises to* L. *of* BERNARD.) You know, Bernard, (*Looking at the third door.*) I've never seen a girl freshly bathed before. . . . Lovely!
BERNARD. I must say Janet's very special.
ROBERT. Delightful. . . . Judith's the one for me, really marvelous. . . . I've rather fallen for Lufthansa.
BERNARD. (*One foot on arm of armchair.*) Have you really?—No, I prefer Jacqueline.
ROBERT. She's very charming too. . . . It's a difficult choice. . . . But we've no time to grade them. You'd better go and tell her the bath's free. And tell her I've given up my turn for her.
BERNARD. You tell her. I'll check that everything's all right in the bathroom. (*Looks in at the bathroom while* ROBERT *knocks on the door of the* D. L. *bedroom.*)
JACQUELINE. (*Off.*) What is it?

ROBERT. It's me, Robert.

JACQUELINE. (*Off.*) What do you want?

ROBERT. You can have my turn in the bathroom.

JACQUELINE. (*Off.*) I don't want it now.

BERNARD. (*Crosses to between table and chair* L.) All clear.

ROBERT. All clear. . . .

JACQUELINE. (*Entering dressed in negligee.*) You've changed your mind? (ROBERT *peers at her seductively.* BERNARD *reproves him silently.*)

BERNARD. Darling, the whole thing was just a joke.

JACQUELINE. I think you are both horrid. Why didn't you tell me it was a joke? I might have understood.

ROBERT. But then it wouldn't have been so funny for us, would it? You wouldn't have been annoyed.

JACQUELINE. It amuses you, does it? To see me getting annoyed?

BERNARD. Yes—no. It amuses me to see Robert being amused because . . . because . . .

JACQUELINE. Because I'm annoyed.

BERNARD. No. That can't be right.

ROBERT. (*Crosses* R.) I really am extremely sorry.

BERNARD. (*Crosses to her.*) And so am I. . . . Please, Jacqueline. (*Kisses her.*)

JACQUELINE. (*Softening.*) Well, well, all right. . . . (*Up to bathroom.*) Bernard, I do wish you'd marry me.

BERNARD. But of course I will marry you in time.

JACQUELINE. (*To* ROBERT.) Don't you think he ought to?

ROBERT. I don't think he deserves you.

JACQUELINE. If you were in his place, wouldn't you marry me at once?

ROBERT. At once. I wouldn't waste a moment.

JACQUELINE. There you are, you see. We see things in you that you can't.

BERNARD. What things?

JACQUELINE. You're just made for marriage.

BERNARD. Me?

JACQUELINE. Of course you are. You hate delays and complications. You like everything to be nice and smooth. You're much too nervous to live by yourself.

ROBERT. She's right, she's absolutely right.

JACQUELINE. Of course I'm right. You're the type of man who needs just one woman. You'd make a marvelous husband. And you know why? Because you're honest. (BERNARD *breaks* D. L.) And that's why I love you. We could be very happy together.

BERNARD. (*Breaks up.*) But we are already.

JACQUELINE. You wait until we're married. You'll notice the difference. (*Exits into the bathroom.*)

BERNARD. (*Crosses* R. *of table to below it and* L. ROBERT *sits desk chair.*) Well, of course another day like this will kill me. (*To armchair and sits.*) I don't understand how you can look so calm about it all.

ROBERT. Perfect control, old man, that's all. And maybe it's because I've led a sheltered life. I'm really very innocent, you know. I've probably still got a guardian angel or something hovering over me. Now if I were you with all your problems, I'd count on someone else. (JUDITH *enters.*) Why not try Mahomet—he's probably used to this sort of situation . . . and start now. (JUDITH *is closing door facing upstage.*)

BERNARD. (*To* L. *of her.*) Who are you? . . . how are you? Darling, it's so lovely to see you.

JUDITH. Bernard, I want to talk to you.

BERNARD. Of course. But what's the matter? You don't look yourself.

ROBERT. (*Crosses onto rostrum, to her* R.) Are you all right?

JUDITH. As a matter of fact, I'm not.

BERNARD. But what is it, my darling?

ROBERT. She must be tired. . . . Why don't you go and lie down?

BERNARD. (*Crosses* L., *then* D. R.) Good idea . . . in here—in here. (*Leading her toward the main bedroom* D. R.)

JUDITH. (D. R.) No. Please leave me alone. I'm afraid I haven't been very honest with you, Bernard. I've deceived you.

BERNARD. Deceived me?

JUDITH. Yes. And I've come back to tell you that I can't go on living with you.

BERNARD. But, darling, we all have little secrets, you know. I mean, there are all sorts of little things that I haven't told you perhaps.

ROBERT. (*To L. of them.*) . . . Perhaps.

JUDITH. (*To ROBERT.*) You keep out of this. It's all your fault.

ROBERT. My fault?

BERNARD. His fault?

JUDITH. Yes, I've grown very fond of your friend.

BERNARD. Him?

ROBERT. Me?

JUDITH. Yes, you. (*To BERNARD.*) That's why I've got to talk to you.

BERNARD. But, darling, that's wonderful. I'm very fond of him too.

JUDITH. I know. And he comes from Aix—you were at school together.

ROBERT. Excuse me, Judith, did . . .

JUDITH. Do keep quiet. You don't know anything.

BERNARD. Yes. Do keep out of this, old man. It's got nothing to do with you.

ROBERT. Forgive me . . . but I do have a slight interest in what's going on.

JUDITH. I kissed him. (ROBERT *lifts desk chair in defense.*)

BERNARD. (*To ROBERT.*) She kissed you?

ROBERT. I'm not saying anything . . . well, except to say it was all an accident.

JUDITH. Only the first one.

BERNARD. The what?

JUDITH. I love him.

ROBERT. You love me?

JUDITH. Yes.

BERNARD. *Him?* Old Robert?

JUDITH. Yes. . . . I'm sorry, but I have to admit it.

BERNARD. Well . . . I must say . . . it's all a bit sudden.

ROBERT. (*Turning away* U. *to above armchair.*) It wasn't my fault.

JUDITH. No. I kissed him because I thought he was you . . . seeing him from behind. (BERNARD *looks at* ROBERT *then studies his own rear.*) . . . and afterwards . . . well, he wanted me to kiss him again.

ROBERT Yes, I can't deny it.

JUDITH. And I liked it. . . . I love him, Bernard.

BERNARD. (*To* ROBERT.) What about you?

ROBERT. Well . . . as a matter of fact, Bernard, I'm really rather smitten.

JUDITH. (*Delighted.*) You are?

ROBERT. I'm schmitten—I'm smitten.

BERNARD. No problem then . . . it just remains for me to offer you my congratulations.

JUDITH. You don't mind?

BERNARD. Well, of course my heart is absolutely shattered . . . but we were at school together, after all. (*Shakes his hand as an afterthought, returns to kiss him on both cheeks. Then breaks to desk.*) You give him a kiss and that might cheer me up.

JUDITH. (*Crosses to* ROBERT. *In* ROBERT'S *arms.*) Robert . . . darling.

(JACQUELINE *enters from bathroom to above chair* L.)

ROBERT. Judith . . . (JACQUELINE *above table.*)

JUDITH. (C. *to* ROBERT.) Who's this?

ROBERT. Goodbye, Bernard. (*Dashes to front door— opens it three times, each time* BERNARD *slams it—frog- marches him back to* C. BERNARD *to* JUDITH'S R.)

JACQUELINE. (L. *to* BERNARD.) Who's that?

BERNARD. Who's who? Me. Oh yes . . . it's . . . er . . . it's Robert's fiancée.

ROBERT. (L. C.) Yes. Robert's fiancée.

JUDITH. (*Overcome.*) Robert! Darling!

JACQUELINE. Congratulations, Robert.

JUDITH. If you only knew how happy I am. . . .

JACQUELINE. Yes. I'm sure you are . . . and I see you're also in the airline business.

JUDITH. I work for Lufthansa.

JACQUELINE. I work for Air-France.

ROBERT. Quite a coincidence.

JACQUELINE. Yes. . . . Are you resting between flights?

BERNARD. Yes, she is between flights, but not resting.

JACQUELINE. We're sisters of a kind then.

BERNARD. Of a kind, yes.

JACQUELINE. Well then, what brings you here at this time of night?

JUDITH. Well, you see . . . I came here to see . . .

ROBERT. Yes . . . you see . . . she came here to see because I am her fian*ecc*, didn't she?

BERNARD. She did. That's exactly what she did.

JUDITH. Oh, no! Not at all. What happened was that . . . (ROBERT *kisses her to shut her up.*) I came here . . . (ROBERT *kisses her to shut her up.*) I came here . . . (ROBERT *kisses her to shut her up.*)

ROBERT. No . . . no . . . no. I could do this all night. It can't really matter.

JACQUELINE. But why didn't you tell me you were engaged?

ROBERT. Er . . . me? Tell *you?*

JACQUELINE. You're so secretive.

JUDITH. Not really. You see, it's only just happened.

ROBERT. Yes . . . just now.

BERNARD. Not five minutes ago!

JACQUELINE. Well, you've been very quick about it. Just time for me to go into the bathroom, have a bath, and—whoops! There you are engaged.

ROBERT. Whoops! There we are, engaged.

BERNARD. (*Takes desk chair back to desk.*) He's very swift, is Robert.

JACQUELINE. (*To* JUDITH.) Where did you meet him?

JUDITH. Here.

JACQUELINE. (*Crosses between armchair and table to* R. *of* JUDITH.) Oh, I see! You came here in the middle of the night to meet your fiancé, not knowing if he'd be here as you'd never met him before—is that it?

BERNARD. Why don't you girls discuss this some other time? Only one thing is clear to me and that is that they are in love. No point in trying to find out why. We'd never get to the end of it.

JACQUELINE. As you will. Anyway—my congratulations again.

JUDITH. Thank you. I hope *you* find someone so . . .

JACQUELINE. Easily?

JUDITH. No . . . someone so sweet as my Robert.

JACQUELINE. Oh! But I have, haven't I, Bernard darling?

BERNARD. Yes, of course.

JUDITH. What?

BERNARD. Well, it's rather difficult to explain.

ROBERT. And there isn't much time. (*Takes* JUDITH's *arm and moves away but her arm slips through his as he moves.*)

JUDITH. Are you engaged to Bernard?

JACQUELINE. Of course I am.

BERNARD. (*Crosses to* JUDITH.) Really, Judith dear. There's no point in going into all that.

ROBERT. No. No point at all. You see, I had something to tell you too. (*Takes* JUDITH's *hand and swings her above him to his left.*) Now what was it? Oh yes . . . as soon as I saw them, I just knew they were very much taken with one another . . .

JUDITH. But how could you know?

JACQUELINE. And I don't see what business it is of yours.

BERNARD. He's always interfering!

ROBERT. Now look here!

JUDITH. (*Breaks* D. L.) You keep quiet! Now then . . . when I was engaged to Bernard . . .

JACQUELINE. (*Breaks down* R.) When you what?

BERNARD. (*To* JACQUELINE—*takes her hand.*) Wait? Let me explain. I was engaged to her, before I became engaged to you.

JACQUELINE. Oh, yes. . . . And then what happened? (ROBERT *is* L. *of armchair—desperately listening.*)

BERNARD. Then . . . then . . . then? (*Turns to* ROBERT *for support.* ROBERT *bows his head.*)

JACQUELINE. Then?

BERNARD. Well, then I suddenly realized that she really loved Robert.

ROBERT. (*Breaks* D. C., *shakes* BERNARD'S *hand.*) That's it—that's absolutely it!

JUDITH. But you didn't know me before. It's only afterwards that I . . .

BERNARD. Please! Please let's not go into all the befores and "afters." What's done is done. The past is the past. There's only one thing is certain, and that's that you are in love. And I'd noticed that, hadn't I . . . ? (*To* JACQUELINE) So I became engaged to her.

JACQUELINE. To who? (ROBERT *sits* L. *arm of armchair.*)

BERNARD. (*To* JUDITH. *To* JACQUELINE.) To you. . . . (*To* JUDITH.) So I shouldn't be jilted . . . (*To* JACQUELINE.) by her!

JACQUELINE. I still don't understand.

BERNARD. But it's perfectly clear . . . isn't it, Robert?

ROBERT. Crystal!

JUDITH. (*Sits* L. *of table.*) And to think I felt guilty! And you were engaged all the time!

JACQUELINE. But of course he was. We've been engaged for ages . . . or else he's a liar.

BERNARD. Me? A liar? (*To* ROBERT.) You tell her, Robert! (ROBERT *rises, above armchair to* JACQUELINE *as if to speak—continues moves* D. R. *of armchair and sits again in armchair.*) There you are, you see? Here's my dearest and oldest friend speaking up for me. And he knows me. He understands. . . .

JACQUELINE. I don't understand anything.

BERNARD. But it's so simple.

JUDITH. Explain it then.

BERNARD. (*Crosses to above table.*) But there's nothing to explain. It's just a question of answering yes or no. (*To* JUDITH.) Are you engaged to Robert?

JUDITH. . . . Yes.

BERNARD. Good. (*To* ROBERT.) Are you engaged to Judith?

ROBERT. Well . . . you see . . . the point is . . .

BERNARD. Yes or no?

ROBERT. Yes.

BERNARD. Good. Splendid. Who else is there? (*Crosses to* U. L. *bedroom, as if to open it, stops in time and crosses* R. *to* JACQUELINE.)

JACQUELINE. Yes . . . of course.

BERNARD. There we are then. (*Points to himself.*) I'm engaged. (*To* JACQUELINE.) You're engaged. And we're engaged to each other. (*To* ROBERT *and* JUDITH.) And they're engaged to each other. And that's all there is to it.

BERTHA. (*Enters from kitchen.*) I've got to talk to you, sir.

BERNARD. (*Sits on table.*) I'm engaged!

BERTHA. (U. C.) It's now or never.

BERNARD. (*Rises, crosses to foot of rostrum.*) I will not be given orders. . . .

JACQUELINE. Oh, come on, darling. . . . For Heaven's sake, don't start arguing with Bertha this time of night.

BERTHA. She's quite right—don't start arguing with— (*Suddenly takes in both* JACQUELINE *and* JUDITH.) Do these ladies know each other?

BERNARD. Of course they know each other. This is Mr. Robert's fiancée—HIS fiancée.

ROBERT. MY fiancée, Bertha.

BERTHA. That was quick. But I always said he was a champion.

BERNARD. And this is my fian . . .

BERTHA. I know . . . I know . . . (*Exits muttering to kitchen.*)

JACQUELINE. (*To* D. L. *bedroom, below table.*) Do come along, Bernard darling. . . . I'm exhausted.

BERNARD. (*Above table.*) Coming right now, my dear.

JUDITH. (*Crossing to* D. R. *bedroom above armchair.*) And you'll come and kiss me good night, Robert darling. I mean, it's all right now we're engaged.

ROBERT. (*Rises—to* R.) What a splendid idea.

JACQUELINE. Good night, all, then.

JUDITH. Good night. We'll have a lovely gossip in the morning.

JACQUELINE. Yes. Let's do that, in the morning. . . . Good night. (BERNARD *following* JACQUELINE. ROBERT *following* JUDITH.)

JUDITH. Good night.

(*The* GIRLS *exit just as* BERTHA *enters carrying her coat and suitcase to front door.*)

BERNARD. (*To* U. L.) Where are you going?

BERTHA. I'm giving in my notice.

BERNARD. You can't do that, Bertha, I'll do anything. I'll increase your wages . . . I'll . . .

BERTHA. How much?

BERNARD. We'll work it out.

BERTHA. Twenty per cent.

BERNARD. Anything you like . . . but you can't leave me. I need you, Bertha.

ROBERT. (*At* U. *end of desk.*) We all need you, Bertha. What a very charming hat.

BERTHA. Well, I'll think about it . . . but it still won't be easy . . . (ROBERT *crosses to her on rostrum.*) —not even with a wage increase. I still think three women in one flat is too much to cope with.

ROBERT. But we're changing all that.
BERNARD. It's all over, Bertha. We've reformed.

(*Enter* JANET *from the* U. L. *bedroom.*)

JANET. Darling, aren't you ever coming to bed?
BERNARD. (*Crosses to her.*) Just coming, darling.
BERTHA. (*Whispers.*) You said that to the other one—in there.
BERNARD. (*Crosses back to* BERTHA.) Be quiet.
JANET. (*At* U. L. *door.*) Do stop whispering and hopping about.
BERTHA. Here's a letter for you—from America. (*Hands letter to* JANET *who crosses to armchair, sits left arm.*)
BERNARD. Why don't you read it in bed?
JANET. No, I want to read it here.
BERNARD. Do read it in bed.
JANET. I'll read it here.
ROBERT. I can't read it. It's all in American.
JANET. For heaven's sake!
BERNARD. (U. L. *of rostrum.*) What is it?
JANET. I don't know how to tell you.
BERNARD. Don't be shy. You are my fiancée, you know.
BERTHA. Here we go again! Another five per cent or I'm off.
BERNARD. (*Crosses to* BERTHA.) Please, Bertha. Stay where you are!
JANET. I can't believe it, it's too marvelous!
BERNARD. (*Crosses to* U. L. *of rostrum.*) What is?
JANET. I'm in love!
BERNARD. I know.
JANET. But not with you, sweetie, not any more. I like you, I like you a lot . . . but it's not good enough. I'm going to have to leave you.
BERTHA. You're going?
JANET. I must.
BERTHA. Then I'll stay.

JANET. It's this guy I met on the Mexico run. He wanted to make his first million before he married me—

ROBERT. Well?

JANET. He's made it.

ROBERT. No!

JANET. (*Rises to* U. L. *door.*) Yes.

BERNARD. Do you mean to tell me you had two men in your life at the same time?

JANET. No, honey, no!

BERNARD. Thank goodness for that!

JANET. Three. I was engaged to another guy in Los Angeles— I suppose I'll have to drop him now.

BERTHA. Why?

JANET. I belong to the man who wants to marry me quickest.

BERNARD. But you can't go off like this. It's not so simple as that.

JANET. Yes, it's quite simple. There's a plane leaving at midnight—local time. I'll ask if I can take a friend's place and when I get home I'll resign from my job. A married life is what I want—I'm sorry, Bernard. (*Exits into* U. L. *bedroom.*)

BERTHA. Now let's just get this straight. You've just got the one fiancée now—Miss Jacqueline, right?

BERNARD. Right.

BERTHA. And you'll take the German off his hands, right?

ROBERT. Right.

BERTHA. Then I'll stay. And with twenty-five per cent on my wages—perhaps things might get a little easier around here. (*Exits into kitchen.* ROBERT *laughs.*)

BERNARD. Do you find it funny?

ROBERT. (U.) Well, you must admit circumstances have forced the solution and made you accept the principle of one woman only.

BERNARD. Yes, I suppose they have. To be honest, I feel relieved.

JACQUELINE. (*At* D. L. *door*.) Please, Bernard. Do come and kiss me good night.

BERNARD. Coming, darling. Just one or two things to tidy up. (*Pretends to busy himself with coffee things*.)

(JACQUELINE *shuts her door. Both* MEN *above armchair*.)

ROBERT. She really is a marvelous girl.

BERNARD. Yes, she is, isn't she! I loved the other two, Robert, but that one I adore.

JUDITH. (*At* D. R. *door*.) Robert . . .

ROBERT. (*Crosses to* D. R. *door*.) Excuse me.

(BERNARD *crosses to* D. L. JUDITH *shuts her door just as* JANET *enters in uniform carrying her luggage*.)

JANET. Here I am, honey. (*Kisses* BERNARD—*crosses to* ROBERT D. R. BERNARD *opens front door*.) I'll think of you from time to time. Goodbye, Robert.

ROBERT. Goodbye, Janet. (*She shakes his hand*.)

JANET. (*Crosses* U. *to door*.) You're a darling—an absolute darling. Goodbye. Say it again.

ROBERT. Goodbye, Janet.

JANET. No. Not that, the other thing.

ROBERT. It's not impossible.

JANET. (*At main door*.) Oh! It's just too kookie. Goodbye. (*Exits*.)

BERNARD. What on earth was all that about?

ROBERT. (*Crosses on to rostrum to* BERNARD.) You say it.

BERNARD. Say what?

ROBERT. It's not impossible.

BERNARD. It's not impossible.

ROBERT. Say it again.

BERNARD. It's not impossible.

ROBERT. No, it doesn't look like a tiny flower to me.

(*The TELEPHONE RINGS.* BERNARD *looks at* ROBERT

and shrugs. ROBERT *shakes his head as* BERNARD *answers the telephone.* ROBERT *crosses to above arm-chair.*)

BERNARD. (*To phone—lifts receiver.*) Hallo? Yes, it's me. . . . Oh! Is it you? (*To* ROBERT.) It's him. It's my friend from the travel agency. Hello. (*At telephone.*) No. . . . No. . . . Thanks. . . . Very good of you. . . . But it doesn't interest me any more. I'm getting married. . . . Yes, I am! . . . No, I'm not joking. . . . What? She's on the Paris-Bombay-Karachi route? No! Thanks . . . no, really. . . . Not even if she's a Hindu. . . . (ROBERT *attracts his attention. To* ROBERT.) You're not going to start all this again, are you?

ROBERT. Why not? A Hindu? I'm not going to let an opportunity like that go by! Go on, take the details.

BERNARD. Robert, think what you're doing.

ROBERT. I am thinking. Go on!

BERNARD. (*Speaking on telephone.*) Hallo. . . . Are you still there? . . . It's for a friend now. Is it all right? Good, I'll pass you over to him. (*Passes receiver to* ROBERT, *crosses to dining room and exits.*)

ROBERT. (*At telephone.*) Hallo? This is the friend speaking. Tell me . . . where can I meet this Hindu lady? Oh! Has she a red spot between her eyes? She has? Wonderful. You also have a Russian girl? Six foot one in high button boots. Good. . . . Wait. (*Sits desk chair.*) I'll take down the details. . . . (*Enter* JUDITH. *To* JUDITH. *Puts phone on* D. *drawer of desk.*) In a minute, darling.

JUDITH. Robert. . . . You know I'm waiting for you.

ROBERT. (*Puts phone in drawer.*) Are you, darling?

JUDITH. Yes. (*Crosses to above him.*) Because I wanted to tell you that now I've met you I'll never be able to sleep until you've kissed me good night.

ROBERT. Wunderbar.

JUDITH. Yes. Just as I'll never again be able to feel

happy on waking without your azure eyes to say good morning to me!

ROBERT. My azure eyes to say good morning!

JUDITH. So as, from tonight, I'll start waiting for you . . . to go to sleep! (*Exits* D. R.)

ROBERT. (*His eye on the door, looks for phone, follows flex into drawer, takes phone out of drawer.*) No, not today, thank you. (*Replaces it in drawer, staring at* D. R. *door. Takes phone out of drawer.*) Hullo—I have changed my mind. I've got somebody else—the girl from all the countries rolled into one, isn't it marvelous? Look, could you do something for me? Could you book me two seats on a plane to Aix-la-Chapelle? Yes? Hallo. Hallo. Damn! We've been cut off. (*Rings off as* BERNARD *returns with a couple of bottles in each hand.*)

BERNARD. (*Above armchair.*) And a good thing too. You don't know how lucky you are. Here, this'll settle your nerves.

ROBERT. Thanks.

(*They move toward the bedrooms—the wrong ones. They realize their mistakes, exchange "Excuse me" and "After you,"* C. *stage, then the TELEPHONE RINGS.*)

BERNARD. Good gracious me.

ROBERT. Another moment and we'd have been in the cart. (*Answers the telephone as* BERNARD *goes into* JACQUELINE'S *room. At phone.*) Hello! . . . We were cut off! Oh, thank you. . . . Can you get me two seats for tomorrow? For Aix-la-Chapelle? You can? Wonderful. . . . On a Boeing? What's that? Ah! It's an airplane. . . . That'll do very nicely. Ten o'clock? Perfect . . . we'll be there. . . . Yes—put some petrol in. (*Hangs up as* JUDITH *enters.*)

JUDITH. Who are you ringing?

ROBERT. Just arranging a little reunion.

JUDITH. Who with?

ROBERT. You, me and your mother. By the statue of Napoleon. (*Leads her towards her bedroom.*)

JUDITH. Not so fast, my darling. You wait there. (*Goes into the bedroom and returns with a pillow.*) We take marriage very seriously in Germany. You can just kiss me and say good night.

(*They kiss and* JUDITH *marches back into her room leaving* ROBERT *clutching the pillow. He is about to protest when* JACQUELINE'S *door opens and she pushes* BERNARD *out—also clutching a pillow and a bottle.*)

JACQUELINE. It's not to be treated flippantly, you know. Especially now we're going to be married. (*Goes back into her bedroom, shutting the door behind her.* BERNARD *grins at* ROBERT.)

BERNARD. You too, old man?

ROBERT. Afraid so. (*They sit* U. R. *on rostrum step.*)

BERNARD. (*Softly.*) Poor old Robert . . .

ROBERT. (*Softly.*) Poor old Bernard . . .

BERNARD. (*Louder.*) When I came out of there I thought . . .

ROBERT. (*Louder.*) When I came out . . .

BERNARD. I was convinced . . . (*Slaps his shoulder, pushing him off stage. They begin to laugh, coming* D.)

ROBERT. You struck me . . . (BERNARD *hits him with his pillow.* ROBERT *hits back.* BERNARD *takes another swipe and the feathers fly. They are back at school— pillow fighting in the dormitory.*)

CURTAIN

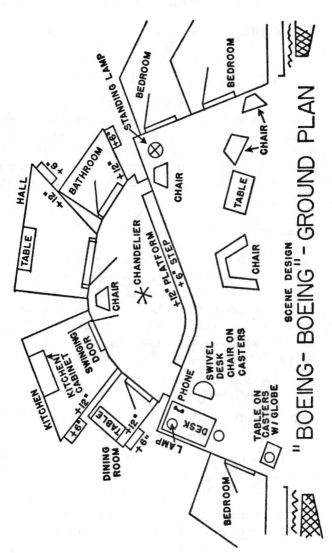

SCENE DESIGN
"BOEING-BOEING"- GROUND PLAN

95